BIBLICAL HEBREW F

By the Same Author

Dan Cohn–Sherbok

BIBLICAL HEBREW
FOR BEGINNERS

First published in Great Britain 1996
Society for Promoting Christian Knowledge
Holy Trinity Church
Marylebone Road
London NW1 4DU

Third impression 2003

British Library Cataloguing-in-Publication Data
A catalogue record for this book is available from
the British Library

ISBN 0-281-04818-5

Typeset by Stephen Ashworth Typesetting, Oxford
at Oxford University Computing Service
Printed in Great Britain by
Antony Rowe Ltd, Chippenham, Wiltshire

For my students

Contents

Contents

Preface

Congratulations! You have made a purchase which will greatly widen your horizons. I promise that if you diligently read through this book, completing all the exercises and checking your answers, you will master the elements of biblical Hebrew. In only a few months you should be able to read the Hebrew Scriptures on your own. All you need is this volume – which is intentionally much simpler and avoids the technical terminology of most grammars – a Hebrew Bible, a dictionary of biblical Hebrew, and an English translation to help you out in case you get stuck.

But – I must emphasize that you can only make progress if you work at biblical Hebrew on a daily basis. You must have a regular routine of study. No more than one hour is required. However, that one hour of study will need to become a regular duty. Ideally you should set aside this study period at the same time each day, perhaps in the morning before going out to work, or in the evening. It doesn't matter when. The important thing is to pace yourself through this book.

We will begin in chapters 1 and 2 by learning the Hebrew alphabet. Chapters 3 to 6 explain how Hebrew words are put together. Then from chapter 7 we will go through the basic elements of the Hebrew language using easy Hebrew examples; this will take us to the end of chapter 14. Starting with chapter 15, we will explore the nature of Hebrew verbs. Then, after this outline of the basic features of biblical Hebrew, you will discover how to use a dictionary in chapter 24. From chapter 25 you will begin reading passages from Genesis and Exodus dealing with such topics as the Garden of Eden, the Flood, Abraham's sacrifice of Isaac, Jacob's vision, Joseph's meeting with his brothers and God's revelation to Moses. Finally, you will be given advice about what parts of the Bible you should read next.

Some students may wish to deepen their understanding of Hebrew by utilizing more complex grammars, for example J. Weingreen's *A Practical Grammar for Classical Hebrew* or

T. Lambdin's *Introduction to Biblical Hebrew*; these books are particularly helpful for those who wish to take advanced courses in biblical Hebrew. But for those who simply wish to read and translate the Bible for themselves, this introduction should be sufficient. It is designed to be simple and straightforward, eliminating the difficult grammatical terminology which often confuses beginning students. As you progress through the chapters you will discover the joys of biblical Hebrew. So let's get started.

CHAPTER ONE

The Alphabet

Let's think about the English language. As a child you first learned to speak English, then in school you learned to write; later you learned the grammatical elements of English. In the process you will have absorbed a number of features of the language without even noticing! For example, English is read and written from left to right. The English alphabet has twenty-six letters which include consonants (such as b, c, d) and vowels (a, e, i, o, u). English has both capital and small letters. English letters are written in the same way no matter where they appear in a word.

Hebrew is different. Unlike English it is read and written from right to left. The Hebrew alphabet has twenty-two letters all of which are consonants. Vowels consist of dots and dashes below and beside the consonants. Hebrew does not have capital letters. Five Hebrew letters have a different form when they appear at the end of the word. So you need to remember that Hebrew is different from English. But that doesn't mean it's harder; in fact it's much simpler in many ways, as we will see.

The first thing you will need to learn is the Hebrew alphabet. Here is a chart of the letters. In the first column is the name of each letter. The next column gives the pronunciation of each letter. The third column lists the letters themselves. The fourth column contains the final forms of five letters.

Letter	Pronunciation	Book Print	Final Form
Aleph	Silent letter	א	
Bet	b as in boy	בּ	
	v as in vine	ב	
Gimmel	g as in girl	ג	
Dalet	d as in door	ד	
Hey	h as in house	ה	
Vav	v as in vine	ו	
Zayin	z as in zebra	ז	

Chet	*ch* as in Ba*ch*	ח	
Tet	*t* as in *t*all	ט	
Yod	*y* as in *y*es	י	
Kaf	*k* as in *k*itty	כּ	ךּ
	ch as in Ba*ch*	כ	ך
Lamed	*l* as in *l*ook	ל	
Mem	*m* as in *m*other	מ	ם
Nun	*n* as in *n*ow	נ	ן
Sameh	*s* as in *s*un	ס	
Ayin	Silent letter	ע	
Pey	*p* as in *p*eople	פּ	ףּ
	f as in *f*ood	פ	ף
Tsade	*ts* as in nu*ts*	צ	ץ
Qof	*k* as in *k*itty	ק	
Resh	*r* as in *r*obin	ר	
Shin	*sh* as in *sh*ape	שׁ	
	s as in *s*un	שׂ	
Tav	*t* as in *t*all	ת	

There are a number of things to be noticed about these letters:

Aleph (א). This letter is silent.

Bet (ב). Be careful to distinguish between a Bet with a dot inside it (בּ) and a Bet without a dot (ב). בּ is pronounced *b* as in *b*oy whereas ב is pronounced *v* as in *v*ine. (In chapter 4 you will learn about the dot.)

Gimmel (ג). There is nothing unusual about this letter: sometimes it has a dot and sometimes it does not. In either case it is pronounced like *g* in girl.

Dalet (ד). Again, there is nothing special about this letter; it is pronounced like *d* as in *d*oor whether it has a dot inside or not.

Hey (ה). The letter ה is pronounced as *h* in *h*ouse, but if it comes at the end of a word without a vowel, it is not pronounced. For example the word תּוֹרָה ends with a ה which is silent.

Vav (ו). The letter ו is pronounced the same way as ב – both are pronounced like *v* as in *v*ine.

Zayin (ז). This letter looks like ו, but it is pronounced like *z* in zebra.

Chet (ח). This letter should not be confused with the letter Hey (ה). It is pronounced like *ch* in the word Ba*ch*.

Tet (ט). There is nothing unusual about this letter. It is pronounced like *t* in the word *t*all with or without a dot inside.

Yod (י). This letter is pronounced like *y* in the word *y*es whether it has a dot or not. It should not be confused with the letter Vav (ו).

Kaf (כ). There are two forms of this letter: when it appears with a dot (כּ) it is pronounced like *k* in *k*itty. When it appears without a dot (כ), it is pronounced like *ch* in the word Ba*ch*. Thus the letters ח and כ are pronounced the same. You should be careful not to confuse the letter Bet (ב) with the letter Kaf (כ). This letter also has a different form when it appears at the end of the word: ך with a dot (when it is pronounced like *k* in the word *k*itty) or ך (when it is pronounced like *ch* in the word Ba*ch*). Be careful not to confuse this final form with the letter Dalet (ד).

Lamed (ל). There is nothing to note about this letter: it is pronounced like *l* in the word *l*ook.

Mem (מ). This letter is pronounced like *m* in the word *m*other. When it is at the end of a word it has a different form: ם.

Nun (נ). This letter is pronounced like *n* in the word *n*ow. Do not confuse this with the letter Kaf (כ). At the end of a word it has the form ן. Do not confuse it with the letter Vav (ו).

Samech (ס). Be careful not to confuse this letter with the final Mem (ם). It is pronounced like *s* in the word *s*un.

Ayin (ע). Like the letter Aleph, the Ayin is silent.

Pey (פ). This letter takes two forms. When it has a dot פּ, it is pronounced like *p* in the word *p*eople. Without a dot (פ), it is pronounced like *f* in the word *f*ood. It also has a different form at the end of a word: ף. With a dot ףּ, it is pronounced like *p* in the word *p*eople; without a dot ף, it is pronounced like *f* in the word *f*ood.

Tsade (צ). This letter is pronounced like *ts* in the word nu*ts*. When it appears at the end of a word it has a different form: ץ.

Qof (ק). This letter is pronounced like *k* in the word *k*itty. Thus it is pronounced the same way as the Kaf with a dot (כּ).

Resh (ר). Do not confuse this letter with a Dalet (ד). It is pronounced like *r* in the word *r*obin.

Shin (ש). This letter has two forms. When it has a dot on the right, שׁ, it is pronounced like *sh* in the word *sh*ape. When it has a dot on the left, שׂ, it is pronounced like *s* in the word *s*un. Thus the שׂ and the Samech ס are pronounced the same way.

Tav (ת). This letter is pronounced *t* as in *t*all whether it has a dot

3

or not. Be careful not to confuse this letter with a Chet ח.

From now on you will be writing Hebrew. But of course it would be difficult to produce letters just as they are printed in books. You will need to use a much simpler form of the letters. To help you do this, I have included the following chart. In the first column are the letters as they appear in books; in the second column are written letters. As you can see, they can be made by using a simple stroke of the pen.

א	א
בּ ב	בּ ב
ג	ג
ד	ד
ה	ה
ו	ו
ז	ז
ח	ח
ט	ט
י	י
כ ך כ ך	כּ ך

ל	ל
מ ם	מ ם
נ ן	נ ן
ס	ס
ע	ע
פ ף פ ף	פּ ף פ ף
צ ץ	צ ץ
ק	ק
ר	ר
שׁ שׂ	שׁ שׂ
ת	ת

4

Exercise 1

Now that you have learned the letters of the Hebrew alphabet, you should practise writing them. Take a lined piece of paper, and write the alphabet twice. Remember to include the final forms of the letters.

Exercise 2

Here is the first verse of Genesis, but with the vowels left out. This is what you will find on Torah scrolls used in synagogues. Believe it or not, the vowels are omitted! That makes it very hard to read, but at this stage it will be easier to write out, although the Hebrew we will be learning in this book does include vowels as well as consonants. For this exercise, try writing out this verse of Genesis:

בראשית ברא אלהים את השמים ואת הארץ

CHAPTER TWO

The Vowels

Let us think for a moment about the way English is written. All the letters – both consonants and vowels – are placed on the same line. For example the word *cat* contains two consonants, *c* and *t*, and one vowel, *a*. The consonants and the vowels are placed one after the other: *cat*. This is true of all English words.

Hebrew, however, follows a different pattern. The consonants, which we have just learned, are placed one after the other just as in English, but Hebrew is written from right to left. The vowels are placed either under the consonants or alongside them. We now need to learn what these vowels are.

There are eight vowels in Hebrew: column 1 is the name of each vowel; column 2 is the vowel placed under or alongside a consonant (which throughout this book is represented as X); column 3 is the sound of the vowel:

Qames	X̤	*a* as in c*a*r
Patah	X̱	*a* as in c*a*r
Hireq	X or ʾX	*ee* as in b*ee*
Sere	X or ʾX	*ay* as in h*ay*
Segol	X̤	*eh* as in b*e*d
Holem	Ẋ or ẊX	*o* as in r*o*pe
Qibbus	X̤	*oo* as in p*oo*l
Sureq	ẊX	*oo* as in p*oo*l

There are a number of observations we should make about these vowels:

The Qames (X̤) and the Patah (X̱) are pronounced the same way: like *a* as in c*a*r.

The Hireq has two forms: X and ʾX – they are both pronounced like *ee* as in b*ee*.

The Sere has two forms: X̱ and ʾX̱ – they are both pronounced like *ay* as in h*ay*.

The Holem has two forms: Ẋ and ẊX – they are both pronounced like *o* as in r*o*pe.

The Qibbus (x̣) and the Sureq (וx) are both pronounced like *oo* as in p*oo*l.

There are also three other vowels based on these vowels:

The Hataf Qames x̤ sounds like *o* as in d*o*g.
The Hataf Patah x̤ sounds like *a* as in c*a*r.
The Hataf Segol x̤ sounds like *eh* as in b*e*d.

Note that the Patah and the Hataf Patah are both pronounced the same way: like *a* as in c*a*r. Also, the Segol and the Hataf Segol sound the same: like *eh* as in b*e*d.

That is all there is to it! So we can now put together the consonants and the vowels. Hebrew follows a simple pattern: the consonant is pronounced first, and then the vowel. Here is an example. When the letter Bet (ב) has a Qames (x̤) under it, it appears as בָ. The consonant is pronounced first, and then the vowel. So בָ is pronounced *ba*.

Here are some more examples. These are all actual Hebrew words – so already you are beginning to read Hebrew! There are twenty-two, each beginning with a different letter of the Hebrew alphabet.

אָב	(av)	father	לֵב	(layv)	heart
בַּת	(bat)	girl	מָה	(ma)	what
גַּם	(gam)	also	נָא	(na)	I pray
דָּם	(dam)	blood	סוּס	(soos)	horse
הֵם	(haym)	they	עַד	(ad)	until
וַ	(va)	and	פֶּה	(peh)	mouth
זֶה	(zeh)	this	צֹאן	(tson)	flock
חֵן	(chayn)	favour	קוֹל	(kol)	voice
טוֹב	(tov)	good	רַב	(rav)	great
יָד	(yad)	hand	שָׁם	(sham)	there
כֹּל	(kol)	all	תּוֹר	(tor)	turtle-dove

All these words have only one syllable, but, as in English, most Hebrew words consist of more than one syllable. Fortunately, longer Hebrew words are pronounced in the same way as shorter ones: the consonant is pronounced first, then the vowel, then the next consonant, then the vowel, and so forth.

Here are several examples. Each is a real Hebrew word, so again you will be expanding your vocabulary. (Remember, Hebrew goes from right to left and the pattern is consonant, vowel, consonant, vowel, etc.)

אֶבֶן	(ehvehn)	stone	כָּבוֹד	(kavod)	honour
בֶּגֶד	(behgehd)	garment	לָמָה	(lama)	why
גָּדוֹל	(gadol)	big	נָבִיא	(navee)	prophet
דָּבָר	(davar)	word	סֵפֶר	(sayfehr)	book
זָהָב	(zahav)	gold	פַּעַם	(paam)	occurrence
חֹדֶשׁ	(chodehsh)	month	עוֹלָם	(olam)	forever
			קֹדֶשׁ	(kodehsh)	holiness

That's all there is to it.

Exercise 1

You need to practise what you have learned so far. Along with lined paper, you need to purchase a big pack of index cards. Begin by writing all the Hebrew words in this chapter, each on a separate card. On the other side of each card you should write the pronunciation and meaning of each word. This way you will be able to shuffle the cards and test yourself as to the pronunciation and meaning of each new word you learn. Do this in your spare time. You could also ask a friend to quiz you.

Exercise 2

After having written out all the vocabulary words in this chapter, you should be able to recognize most of the consonants and vowels. Exercise 2 is to write out the pronunciation of each of the words listed below. Again, these are real Hebrew words, so add them to your growing list of Hebrew vocabulary. Check your pronunciation with the answers at the end of the book to make sure you have not made any mistakes. And then write each word on a card with the pronunciation and meaning on the back.

1.	אָדוֹן	Lord	11.	כֹּהֵן	priest
2.	בֵּן	son	12.	לֹא	not
3.	גּוֹיִים	peoples	13.	נוֹרָא	awesome
4.	דוֹר	generation	14.	סוּכָּה	booth
5.	הַכֹּל	everything	15.	עָפָר	dust
6.	וְ	and	16.	פֶּסַח	Passover
7.	זֶרַע	seed	17.	צוּר	rock
8.	חוּץ	outside	18.	קֶבֶר	grave
9.	טוּר	row	19.	רִאשׁוֹן	first
10.	יָם	sea	20.	שַׁבָּת	Sabbath

9

Syllables

In all languages words consist of syllables (or sound units). The
vowels determine how many syllables a word has. The word *cat* in
English, for example, has one vowel and consists of one syllable.
Other words, such as *rabbit*, with two vowels, consist of two syllables: *rab+bit*. Longer words, such as *elephant*, with three vowels,
consist of three syllables: *el+e+phant*. Some longer words have even
more syllables.

In words of one syllable, it is obvious where the stress falls: there is
only one sound unit, so it must fall on that syllable. But when there
are two or more syllables, it is unclear where the stress should be.
Take the word *rabbit*. Here the stress falls on the first syllable: *rab*.
But looking at the word, there is no way to know this. Our knowledge of where to stress English words comes from usage. This is
something that foreigners often find puzzling when they begin to
learn English.

Like English, Hebrew contains words of one syllable. We learned
a number of them in the last chapter. In these cases, the stress falls
on the single syllable. But we also learned a number of words with
more than one syllable. How can one know which syllable should be
stressed? In general, Hebrew words are stressed on the last syllable.
But this is not always the case. Sometimes they are stressed on the
next to last syllable. You will be glad to learn that biblical Hebrew
contains little accent marks (originally musical notes) which indicate where the stress falls. So you will never be uncertain where to
stress a word. However, to avoid confusion I have not included them
in this book.

Here are some examples of words which are stressed on the last
syllable:

אִשָּׁה	(eesha)	woman
קָטָן	(katan)	small

The following words are stressed on the next to last syllable indicated by ‹ which will be used in this chapter to help you learn about

syllables:

אֹהֶל	(ohehl)	tent
כֶּסֶף	(kehsehf)	money
עֶצֶם	(ehtsehm)	essence

To help you divide Hebrew words into syllables, you will need to know about two kinds of vowels: Open and Closed (known in most grammars as Long and Short Vowels). So far we have seen that there are eight main vowels. These consist of the Qames (X̤), Patah (X̤), Hireq (X̤ or ׳X̤), Sere (X̤ or ׳X̤), Segol (X̤), Holem (X̊ or ׳X̊), Qibbus (X̤), and Sureq (וX).

The Open Vowels are:

Qames	X̤	*a* as in c*a*r
Sere	X̤ or ׳X̤	*ay* as in h*ay*
Hireq	׳X	*ee* as in b*ee*
Holem	X̊ or וX̊	*o* as in r*o*pe
Sureq	וX	*oo* as in p*oo*l

The Closed Vowels are:

Patah	X̤	*a* as in c*a*r
Segol	X̤	*eh* as in b*e*d
Hireq	X̤	*ee* as in b*ee*
Qames	X̤	*o* as in d*o*g
Qibbus	X̤	*oo* as in p*oo*l

Let us take a good look at these two kinds of vowels. You will see that the Qames (X̤) can be either an Open or Closed Vowel. If it is closed it is pronounced like *o* as in d*o*g. I will explain later how to distinguish between the Open and Closed Qames. The Hireq spelled ׳X is an Open Vowel, but when it is spelled X it is Closed.

I am now going to tell you about a very important principle which governs Open and Closed Vowels. Syllables in Hebrew can either end with a vowel, such as the word לוֹ (to him), or they can end with a consonant, as in the case of עַד (until). If they end with a vowel they are called 'Open Syllables' and generally take Open Vowels. If they end with a consonant, they are Closed Syllables and generally take Closed Vowels.

Let us look first at unstressed syllables. An unstressed Open

Syllable has an Open Vowel (as in the case of נוֹרָא (awesome) where the Holem (וֹX) is an Open Vowel). An unstressed Closed Syllable, on the other hand, has a Closed Vowel (as in the case of אֹהֶל (tent) where the Segol (X) is a Closed Vowel). This, then, is the rule regarding unstressed syllables: Open Syllables which are unstressed end in Open Vowels, Closed Syllables if they are unstressed end in a consonant and contain a Closed Vowel. Here are some examples which illustrate this rule:

- The word דָּוִד (David) is composed of two syllables. The first (דָּ) is an unstressed Open Syllable which ends in the Open Vowel Qames (X).

- The word חֹדֶשׁ (month) has two syllables. The second syllable (דֶשׁ) is an unstressed Closed Syllable which contains the Closed Vowel Segol (X).

But what happens if either the Open or Closed Syllable is stressed? In such cases the Open Syllable can take either an Open Vowel or a Closed Vowel. Similarly, a stressed Closed Syllable can take either a Closed Vowel or an Open Vowel. This means that when the stress falls on Open and Closed Syllables, they can take the opposite vowel than they would if they were unstressed. Let me give you some examples:

- The word אֵם (mother) consists of a stressed Closed Syllable. If it were unstressed, it would take a Closed Vowel. But because it is stressed, it takes the Open Vowel Sere (X).

- The word יוֹסֵף (Joseph) consists of two syllables. The first (יוֹ) is an unstressed Open Syllable and ends in the Open Vowel Holem (וֹX). The second syllable סֵף is a stressed Closed Syllable. If it were unstressed, it would take a Closed Vowel, but because it is stressed it here takes the Open Vowel Sere (X).

- The word עֶרֶב (evening) contains two syllables. The first (עֶ) is a stressed Open Syllable. If it were unstressed, it would take an Open Vowel, but because it is stressed, it here takes the Closed Vowel Segol (X). The second syllable (רֶב) is an unstressed Closed Syllable and takes the Closed Vowel Segol (X).

There is one final point in this connection. Remember the Qames can be either an Open Vowel (when it is pronounced *a* as in c*a*r), or a Closed Vowel (when it is pronounced *o* as in d*o*g). In unstressed Open Syllables the Qames is an Open Vowel as in the first syllable (דָּ) of דָּוִד (David). In unstressed Closed Syllables the Qames is a Closed Vowel as in the first syllable (חָכְ) of חָכְמָה (wisdom). However, if the Qames is in a stressed Open or Closed Syllable, it can be either an Open or Closed Vowel. To illustrate this point, let us look at the word בָּקָר (herd), which is composed of two syllables. The first syllable (בָּ) is an unstressed Open Syllable, and so it ends in the Open Vowel Qames. However the second syllable (קָר) is a stressed Closed Syllable, and therefore here has the Open Vowel Qames.

To sum up then, unstressed Open Syllables take Open Vowels, whereas unstressed Closed Syllables take Closed Vowels. However, stressed syllables, both Open and Closed, can take either Open or Closed Vowels.

Exercise 1

Indicate whether the syllables are Open or Closed and whether the vowels are Open or Closed. Here is an example:

בֹּקֶר (morning)

Closed Syllable	Open Syllable
Closed Vowel	Open Vowel
קֶר	בֹּ

1. אֹֽזֶן (ear)
2. זָכַר (he remembered)
3. יָרַשׁ (he inherited)
4. כָּתַב (he wrote)

Exercise 2

Indicate whether the syllables are Open or Closed and whether the vowels are Open or Closed.

1. אֶ֫בֶן   (stone)

2. בֶּ֫גֶד   (garment)

3. יַ֫יִן   (wine)

4. פֶּ֫סַח   (Passover)

5. שַׁ֫חַר   (dawn)

Exercise 3

Here are several Hebrew sentences with stress indicated. See if you can divide the words in these sentences into syllables:

1. ט֫וֹב הַדָּבָ֫ר   The word is good. (Deut. 1.14)

2. לֹא אִ֫ישׁ אֵ֫ל   God is not a man. (Num. 23.19)

3. אֱלֹהִ֫ים בַּשָּׁמַ֫יִם   God is in Heaven. (Eccles. 5.1)

CHAPTER FOUR

The Sheva

So far we have learned about the major Hebrew vowels. But there is one other vowel sound that I want to tell you about. In addition to the Open and Closed Vowels, there is another vowel called the Sheva (X̣). This is a very short vowel sound like the *a* in banana.

In this book I will indicate the Sheva (X̣) by @ to distinguish it from all the other vowel sounds. Thus for example, the word גְּבוּל (border) is pronounced g@vool. Here are some more examples:

כְּמוֹ (like) is pronounced k@mo

פְּרִי (fruit) is pronounced p@ree

צְדָקָה (righteousness) is pronounced ts@daka

There is one peculiarity about the Sheva which makes it different from all the other vowels: there are times when it is not pronounced at all. In these cases, it is silent. You will no doubt want to ask me how you can know when the Sheva is sounded and when it is silent. A good question! There are a number of simple rules which can guide you:

- At the beginning of a word, the Sheva is sounded (as in the examples above). Here are some more:

  יְהוּדָה (Judah) y@hooda

  לְמַעַן (in order that) l@maan

  תְּפִלָּה (prayer) t@feela

- When two Shevas appear in a row (X̣X̣), the first is silent but the second is sounded. Thus the word מִשְׁפְּחוֹת (families) is pronounced meeshp@chot. These are some more examples:

  יִכְתְּבוּ (they shall write) yeecht@voo

  יִשְׁמְרוּ (they shall keep) yeeshm@roo

  מִזְבְּחוֹת (altars) meezb@chot

- When the Sheva is preceded by a Closed Vowel, it closes the syllable and is silent. For example, in the word יִשְׂרָאֵל (Israel) the first syllable (יִשׁ) is a Closed Syllable with the Closed Vowel Hireq (x) and a silent Sheva. Here are other examples:

יִצְחָק (Isaac). The first syllable (יִצְ) is Closed and the Sheva is silent.

מִשְׁפָּט (justice). The first syllable (מִשְׁ) is Closed and the Sheva is silent.

- If the Sheva is preceded by an Open Vowel, it forms a syllable and is sounded as in שׁוֹמְרִים (keepers). Here the first syllable (שׁוֹ) is Open and the vowel is Open. The Sheva which follows this Open Vowel forms the next syllable (מְ) and is sounded. The third syllable is רִים. Here are some more examples:

יוֹשְׁבִים (residents) yosh@veem
שׁוֹפְטִים (judges) shof@teem
הוֹלְכִים (walkers) hol@cheem

There is one final point about the Sheva. You will remember that there are three vowels that are based on the main vowels: Hataf Qames (x), Hataf Patah (x), and Hataf Segol (x). If you look closely you can see that each of these is composed of the Sheva plus a vowel:

Hataf Qames=Qames (x) and Sheva (x)
Hataf Patah=Patah (x) and Sheva (x)
Hataf Segol=Segol (x) and Sheva (x)

These vowels take the place of the Sheva when it is sounded under four letters: א, ה, ח, ע.

These are some examples:
אֱלִיעֶזֶר (Eliezer) ehleeehzehr
הֲרֵי (lo!) haray
חֲלוֹם (dream) chalom
עֲבָדִים (slaves) avadeem

Exercise 1

Here are some words that contain a Sheva. Write the pronunciation of each word. You will need to figure out if the Sheva is sounded or silent to write the correct pronunciation.

1. אַבְרָהָם (Abraham)
2. מִצְוָה (commandment)
3. מַלְכְּךָ (your king)
4. יַלְדָה (girl)
5. עַבְדְּךָ (your servant)
6. תּוֹלְדוֹת (generations)
7. פַּרְעֹה (Pharaoh)
8. מִלְחָמָה (war)
9. מוֹשְׁבוֹת (generations)
10. מַלְכָּה (queen)

11. יִקְבְּרוּ (they shall bury)
12. יִשְׁמְרוּ (they shall keep)
13. מִקְנֶה (cattle)
14. מִדְבָּר (desert)
15. אַרְבַּע (four)
16. שְׁמַרְתֶּם (you kept)
17. בְּלִי (without)
18. יִרְאָה (fear)
19. בְּרָכָה (blessing)

Exercise 2

These are some words that contain either a Hataf Qames (x̱), Hataf Patah (x̱), Hataf Segol (x̟). Write out the pronunciation of each word.

1. אֲנַחְנוּ (we)
2. יַעֲקֹב (Jacob)
3. כַּאֲשֶׁר (as)
4. מוֹעֲדִים (appointed times)
5. מַחֲנוֹת (camps)

6. מַעֲשֶׂה (deed)
7. נָעֳמִי (Naomi)
8. עֲבָדִים (slaves)
9. עֲבוֹדָה (work)

CHAPTER FIVE

The Dot

You will have noticed that many of the Hebrew words you have learned contain dots in some letters. What are they? The first kind of dot appears in six Hebrew letters: Bet (בּ), Gimmel (גּ), Dalet (דּ), Kaf (כּ), Pey (פּ), Tav (תּ), when these letters begin a syllable, as long as they are not preceded by a vowel. Here are some examples:

The letter Bet (בּ):	בֶּגֶד	(garment)
	מִדְבָּר	(desert)
The letter Gimmel (גּ):	גְּבוּל	(border)
	לִנְגֹּף	(to smite)
The letter Dalet (דּ):	דָּבָר	(word)
	יַלְדָּה	(girl)
The letter Kaf (כּ):	כֹּהֵן	(priest)
	בִּרְכַּיִם	(knees)
The letter Pey (פּ):	פֶּסַח	(Passover)
	מִשְׁפָּט	(judgement)
The letter Tav (תּ):	תּוֹרָה	(law)
	פְּלִשְׁתִּי	(Philistine)

Note that in all these examples the letters בּ, גּ, דּ, כּ, פּ, תּ either begin a syllable at the beginning of a word or in the middle of a word. When they begin a word, they are obviously not preceded by a vowel. When they begin a syllable in the middle of a word, they are preceded by a silent Sheva – thus again they are not preceded by a vowel.

However, if any of these letters begins a syllable that is preceded by a vowel, it does not have a dot. Here are some examples:

The letter Bet (ב):	אֶבֶן	(stone)
The letter Gimmel (ג):	רֶגֶל	(foot)
The letter Dalet (ד):	אָדוֹן	(lord)
The letter Kaf (כ):	חָכָם	(wise)
The letter Pey (פ):	יָפֶה	(beautiful)
The letter Tav (ת):	אָתוֹן	(she-ass)

18

Similarly, if any of these letters closes a syllable, it does not have a dot. These are some examples:

The letter Bet (ב):	אַבְרָהָם	(Abraham)
The letter Gimmel (ג):	יִגְדַּל	(he will be great)
The letter Dalet (ד):	מִדְבָּר	(desert)
The letter Kaf (כ):	אָכְלָה	(food)
The letter Pey (פ):	לִפְנֵי	(before)
The letter Tav (ת):	הִתְקַדֵּשׁ	(he sanctified himself)

Now, there is a simple way of remembering the letters: Bet (ב), Gimmel (ג), Dalet (ד), Kaf (כ), Pey (פ), Tav (ת). They are known as the 'B@gad K@fat' letters from the made-up word בְּגַדְכְּפַת. This word does not mean anything, but it should help to remind you what these letters are. Remember: B@gad K@fat!

Besides affecting the B@gad K@fat letters, the dot also is placed in letters to indicate that they need to be doubled. This dot (which looks no different from the dot placed in B@gad K@fat letters) is called the 'doubling dot' and is always preceded by a vowel (unlike a dot in a B@gad K@fat letter which is never preceded by a vowel). Such doubling happens in various situations. For example, when the preposition 'from' (מִן) is joined to the name 'Saul' (שָׁאוּל), מִן שָׁאוּל (from Saul) should become מִנְשָׁאוּל. But the letter Nun (נ) is dropped, and a doubling dot is placed in the letter Shin (שׁ). 'From Saul' therefore becomes מִשָּׁאוּל. Here the doubling dot in the שׁ indicates that it should be doubled so that the word מִשָּׁאוּל should be pronounced as though it were written מִשְׁשָׁאוּל.

You can see then that in some cases the doubling dot is placed in a letter to double it because another letter has disappeared. This is not so strange since the same thing happens in English. For example, the word 'illegal' is derived from the Latin 'inlegal' where the 'n' has disappeared and the letter 'l' has been doubled.

Later we will see that the doubling dot is also placed in letters in some verbs to indicate that the letter should be doubled. For example the word בִּקֵּשׁ (he sought) has a doubling dot in the letter ק to indicate that it should be doubled. Thus the word should be pronounced as though it were בִּקְקֵשׁ.

You might wonder when you come across a letter with a dot, whether the dot doubles the letter or serves some other function. If the dot is in a B@gad K@fat letter which begins a word, or begins a syllable in the middle of a word as long as it is not preceded by a vowel, it does not double the letter. But if the dot is in a letter in the middle of a word and is preceded by a vowel, it doubles the letter. Look at the word קִבֵּל (he received): here the בּ is in the middle of a word and is preceded by the vowel Hireq (X). Thus the בּ is doubled.

You will be relieved to learn that even though doubling dots technically double the letters in which they occur, in fact most people slur over double letters when they pronounce Hebrew. They shouldn't, but they do! As far as the exercises are concerned, you should indicate the correct pronunciation when you write out the transliteration of words that double their letters. But when you actually pronounce them, there is no need to be so careful. You can run them together just as most Hebrew speakers do!

It should be noted that the letters Aleph (א), Hey (ה), Chet (ח), Ayin (ע), Resh (ר) do not take dots. What happens if these letters should be doubled? In such cases a change is made instead to the vowels preceding them. For example if the word 'from' (מִן) were to be linked to the word 'man' (אִישׁ), it would theoretically appear as מִאִּישׁ. But the Aleph (א) cannot take a dot. So the Hireq (X) preceding the Aleph becomes the Open Vowel Sere (X). 'From man' thus becomes מֵאִישׁ. You will need to remember what these five letters are which do not take dots – they are referred to as the 'throaty five' since they were originally sounded in the throat. Remember: א, ה, ח, ע, ר do not take dots!

Sometimes, however, the dot does appear in the letter Hey (ה) but here it has a different function than doubling. Here it is a 'sounding dot'. You will remember that when the letter ה is at the end of a word, it is not pronounced. But in some cases, it needs to be sounded. Whenever this happens, a dot is placed inside it. For example, the word סוּסָה means 'mare'. But 'her mare' is spelled סוּסָהּ where the ה is pronounced since it has a dot inside it.

Exercise 1

Write the pronunciation of each word (none of these dots is doubled):

1. אֶבְיוֹן (poor)
2. אֲדָמָה (land)
3. אֲהָהּ (alas)
4. אַרְבַּה (four)
5. בְּהֵמָה (cattle)
6. בָּחַר (he chose)
7. בַּיִת (house)
8. דָּם (blood)
9. זָכַר (he remembered)
10. כָּבוֹד (glory)

11. מִדְבָּר (desert)
12. מַלְכָּה (queen)
13. מִסְפָּר (number)
14. מִשְׁפַּט (justice)
15. נָכָה (smite)
16. נָפַל (he fell)
17. סֵפֶר (book)
18. פָּנִים (face)
19. תֹּהוּ (desolation)
20. תַּחַת (under)

Exercise 2

Write the pronunciation for each word. (All the dots in letters in
the middle of a word indicate doubling.)

1. אַיֵּה (where)
2. אִשָּׁה (woman)
3. אֵלִיָּהוּ (Elijah)
4. בָּמָה (high place)
5. גִּבּוֹר (hero)
6. הִנֵּה (behold)
7. חִטָּה (wheat)
8. יַבָּשָׁה (dry land)

9. כַּמָּה (how much)
10. כִּסֵּא (seat)
11. לָמָּה (why)
12. מִלָּה (word)
13. מַקֵּל (staff)
14. מִשָּׁם (from there)
15. עַתָּה (now)

CHAPTER SIX

Letters and Marks

We have seen that there are several letters – Aleph (א), Hey (ה), Chet (ח) and Ayin (ע) – which do not take a dot. These letters also do not take a Sheva under them; instead they prefer a Hataf Qames (ֳx), Hatef Patah (ֲx), and Hataf Segol (ֱx). The א generally prefers a Segol (ֶx) as in אֶחָד (one) or a Hataf Segol (ֱx) as in אֱלִיעֶזֶר (Eliezer). The ה, ח, ע, however, often prefer a Patah (ַx) as in הַר (mountain), חַיִּים (life), and עַיִן (eye).

With regard to the Patah, you should note that when a Chet and a Patah (חַ) appear at the end of a word preceded by an Open Vowel, they are pronounced in the reverse order: the Patah is pronounced first and then the Chet. Thus the word רוּחַ is pronounced 'rooach' rather than 'roocha'.

So far you will have seen that the Yod (י) is not pronounced when it forms part of the Hireq (יx) or Sere (יx). The Yod is also linked to two other vowels to produce different sounds:

יַx   is pronounced *ai* as in *ai*sle
יוֹx   is pronounced *oi* as in *oi*l

Thus the word חַי (living) is pronounced 'chai' and the word גּוֹי (nation) is pronounced 'goi'.

As mentioned previously, the Bible contains marks in addition to vowels, which indicate stress. Let's look at the first verse of Genesis:

בְּרֵאשִׁית בָּרָא אֱלֹהִים אֵת הַשָּׁמַיִם וְאֵת הָאָרֶץ:

In the first word בְּרֵאשִׁית there is a mark under the שׁ which indicates that the word is stressed on the last syllable. Similarly, the next word בָּרָא has a mark under the ר to indicate that the stress falls on the last syllable. The third word has a mark under the ה to indicate that the stress falls on the final syllable. This particular mark also divides the sentence into two parts – it is always used to divide Hebrew sentences into two parts. The next word אֵת has a mark under the א to show that the stress falls on the next to last syllable, and the next word הַשָּׁמַיִם has a mark under the מ to indicate where the stress falls. The next word הָאָרֶץ also has a mark under the next to last syllable to show where the word is stressed. There is also a mark at the end of the sentence (:) which acts as a full stop.

In addition to these stress marks, there are a few other marks which are important:

- Some words contain a short horizontal line above a letter to indicate that a 'doubling dot' has been omitted. For example, the word בִּקֵּשׁ (he sought) is spelled with a 'doubling dot' in the ק. However, occasionally the 'doubling dot' is omitted and the word is spelled בִּקֵשׁ where the line over the ק indicates that a 'doubling dot' has been eliminated.

- Frequently in the Bible two words are connected by a dash (־) as in the case of כָּל־אָדָם (any man). In these cases the stress on the first word is omitted. Thus here כָּל becomes an unstressed Closed Syllable with the Closed Vowel Qames.

- A small perpendicular stroke is frequently placed to the left of a vowel to make sure that the vowel is pronounced, rather than neglected in favour of another vowel which is stressed. For example, the word הָאָדָם has the mark ˂ above the ד to indicate that the stress falls on the last syllable. But it also has a perpendicular stroke next to the Qames under the ה to indicate that its Qames should be sounded and not neglected in favour of the Qames under the ד in the final syllable.

- In words which divide a Hebrew sentence into two parts (indicated by the mark ʌ) or in words at the end of a sentence, the vowels sometimes change. For example the word מַיִם (water) is normally spelled with a Patah in the stressed Open Syllable (מַ). But in the middle or at the end of a sentence, the vowel changes to the Open Vowel Qames (X̲) so that the word becomes מָיִם.

Exercise 1

Write the pronunciation of the following words:

1.	אֱדוֹם (Edom)	7.	עֲבוֹדָה (labour)	
2.	אֶחָד (one)	8.	לְמַעַן (in order that)	
3.	אֶרֶץ (earth)	9.	רָחַץ (he washed)	
4.	חַג (festival)	10.	שַׁחַר (dawn)	
5.	הַר (mountain)	11.	רוּחַ (spirit)	
6.	עָם (people)	12.	לוּחַ (tablet)	

Exercise 2

Circle the stress marks in the following verses from Genesis 1.1-2a:

בְּרֵאשִׁית בָּרָא אֱלֹהִים אֵת הַשָּׁמַיִם וְאֵת הָאָרֶץ:

(In the beginning, God created the heavens and the earth)

וְהָאָרֶץ הָיְתָה תֹהוּ וָבֹהוּ וְחֹשֶׁךְ עַל־פְּנֵי תְהוֹם:

(and the earth was without form, and void; and darkness was upon the face of the deep.)

CHAPTER SEVEN

Nouns

You should now be able to read most Hebrew words. It is time to look at the building blocks of the Hebrew language. Let us look first at nouns. Remember: a noun is the name of a person, place or thing. In Hebrew nouns are either masculine or feminine. Obviously a word such as מֶלֶךְ (king) is masculine whereas a word like מַלְכָּה (queen) is feminine. Other words, however, such as בַּיִת (house) which is masculine and מִשְׁפָּחָה (family) which is feminine are arbitrarily designated as one gender or the other. Here are some masculine nouns:

סוּס	horse	כּוֹכָב	star
שִׁיר	song	גּוֹי	nation

These are some feminine nouns:

סוּסָה	mare	בְּרָכָה	blessing
מְנוֹרָה	candelabra	מִצְוָה	commandment

Looking at this list, you can see that feminine nouns follow a similar pattern – they end in הָ. This is not universally the case, but in general you will find most feminine nouns have this ending, or the ending ת as in the word בַּת (daughter). There are, however, no characteristic endings for masculine nouns. The only general principle to follow is that if a noun does end in הָ or ת it is probably feminine. To be sure, you will need to look up the gender of a noun in the dictionary.

The nouns listed so far are all singular. What about plural nouns? Let us think first about plural masculine nouns. Masculine nouns are generally made plural by adding the ending ים to the singular form. Thus דּוֹד (uncle) becomes דּוֹדִים (uncles); סוּס (horse) becomes סוּסִים (horses); שִׁיר (song) becomes שִׁירִים (songs). However, in many cases the vowels underneath masculine nouns change when ים is added. This happens because of the rhythm of speech. Here are some examples:

25

אָח	brother	אַחִים	brothers
בֵּן	son	בָּנִים	sons
דָּבָר	word	דְּבָרִים	words
הַר	mountain	הָרִים	mountains
יוֹם	day	יָמִים	days
מֶלֶךְ	king	מְלָכִים	kings
עֶבֶד	servant	עֲבָדִים	servants

Feminine plural nouns are formed by adding וֹת. If feminine nouns end in הָx, the ה is dropped before וֹת is added. As with masculine nouns, the vowels often undergo changes when the extra syllable וֹת is added to singular nouns. Again, this occurs because of the rhythm of speech. Here are some examples:

בְּהֵמָה	animal	בְּהֵמוֹת	animals
מִשְׁפָּחָה	family	מִשְׁפָּחוֹת	families
נַעֲרָה	young woman	נְעָרוֹת	young women

This pattern of change is not universal. There are some masculine nouns which take the feminine plural form וֹת such as the word אָב (father) which becomes אָבוֹת (fathers). Similarly, some feminine nouns take the masculine plural ending יםx such as the feminine noun עִיר (city) which becomes עָרִים (cities).

It should be noted as well that there are some nouns which undergo irregular changes when they become plural. Here are some examples:

אִישׁ	man	אֲנָשִׁים	men
אִשָּׁה	woman	נָשִׁים	women

So far all the nouns you have learned have been unspecific: a king, a horse, etc. But how does one write *the* king, *the* horse, *the* man? In English the word 'a' or 'the' is placed before a noun. But in Hebrew there is another method. To make a word definite, you need to attach the prefix הַ to the noun and place a dot in the first letter of the word. Thus 'a king' מֶלֶךְ becomes הַמֶּלֶךְ. Remember the dot: it has to be placed in the first letter of the word (as long as the letter will accept a dot). The letters א, ה, ח, ע, ר do not take dots. We will learn in a moment what to do about these letters. First, here are some examples of words made definite:

סוּס	horse	הַסּוּס	the horse

26

בֵּן a son   הַבֵּן the son
יוֹם a day   הַיּוֹם the day

Plural nouns are made definite in the same way: the prefix הַ is added to plural nouns, and a dot is placed in the first letter of the word. Again, here are some examples:

מְלָכִים kings   הַמְּלָכִים the kings
בְּהֵמוֹת animals   הַבְּהֵמוֹת the animals
נְעָרוֹת young women   הַנְּעָרוֹת the young women

What about the letters that will not take dots? In such cases, the vowel under the ה is altered to either a Qames (X̱) or a Segol (X̱). Here are some examples:

אָדָם man   הָאָדָם the man
עִיר city   הָעִיר the city
עָפָר dust   הֶעָפָר the dust

The same procedure applies to plural nouns. If the first letter does not take a dot, then the vowel under the ה is either a Qames (X̱) or a Segol (X̱). Here are some examples:

הָרִים mountain   הֶהָרִים the mountains
רָאשִׁים heads   הָרָאשִׁים the heads

Exercise 1

Translate the following words:

נַעַר	1.	עַמִּים	14.
הַדָּבָר	2.	אֲרָצוֹת	15.
הַבַּיִת	3.	מִשְׁפָּחוֹת	16.
עִיר	4.	הַבְּהֵמוֹת	17.
הֶעָרִים	5.	עַם	18.
אִישׁ	6.	הָרֹאשׁ	19.
דָּוִד	7.	הָעַיִן	20.
הַמֶּלֶךְ	8.	הֶעָפָר	21.
הַבֵּן	9.	הָהָר	22.
אָבוֹת	10.	הָאוֹר	23.
אַחִים	11.	הַחֹשֶׁךְ	24.
הֶהָרִים	12.	הָרֶגֶל	25.
הַמְּלָכִים	13.		

Exercise 2

Here are some Hebrew sentences. I have given the translation of all the words in the sentences except for some nouns which I have put in parentheses. See if you can find the missing noun in each sentence in the vocabulary list, and then give a translation of the sentence.

1. אֶחָד [יְהֹוָה] —— is one. (Deut. 6.4)
2. וַ[הַמֶּלֶךְ] שְׁלֹמֹה בָּרוּךְ And the ——, Solomon, will be blessed. (1 Kings 2.45)
3. בִּי [מְלָכִים] יִמְלֹכוּ By me —— reign. (Prov. 8.15)
4. וְשָׁם [אִשָּׁה] גְדוֹלָה A wealthy —— was there. (2 Kings. 4.8)

CHAPTER EIGHT

Adjectives

In English, adjectives are placed before the words they describe, as in 'the *good* king'. In addition, the same adjective is used to describe masculine and feminine as well as singular and plural nouns. Thus the adjective 'good' is used as follows: 'a *good* king'; 'a *good* queen'; '*good* kings'; '*good* queens'.

In Hebrew, however, adjectives follow the nouns they describe as in מֶלֶךְ טוֹב (a good king). Furthermore, every Hebrew adjective takes four forms which correspond to the four types of Hebrew nouns: masculine singular, feminine singular, masculine plural, feminine plural. Hebrew adjectives therefore must match the type of nouns they describe – they must agree in both number and gender. You will be glad to know that Hebrew adjectives follow the same pattern as the nouns.

Let us think back to the pattern of nouns. They generally follow this sequence:

Nouns

| Masculine Singular | XXX | Masculine Plural | XXXים |
| Feminine Singular | XXXה | Feminine Plural | XXXוֹת |

Here is an example:

| מֶלֶךְ king | מְלָכִים kings |
| מַלְכָּה queen | מְלָכוֹת queens |

Adjectives, too, follow the same pattern:

Adjectives

| Masculine Singular | XXX | Masculine Plural | XXXים |
| Feminine Singular | XXXה | Feminine Plural | XXXוֹת |

Here are some examples:

טוֹב good

| Masculine Singular | טוֹב | Masculine Plural | טוֹבִים |
| Feminine Singular | טוֹבָה | Feminine Plural | טוֹבוֹת |

29

גָּדוֹל big

Masculine Singular	גָּדוֹל	Masculine Plural	גְּדוֹלִים
Feminine Singular	גְּדוֹלָה	Feminine Plural	גְּדוֹלוֹת

חָכָם wise

Masculine Singular	חָכָם	Masculine Plural	חֲכָמִים
Feminine Singular	חֲכָמָה	Feminine Plural	חֲכָמוֹת

Adjectives and the nouns they describe thus follow this pattern:

	Noun	+	Adjective
Masculine Singular	XXX	+	XXX
Feminine Singular	XXXָה	+	XXXָה
Masculine Plural	XXXִים	+	XXXִים
Feminine Plural	XXXוֹת	+	XXXוֹת

Here is an example using king and queen:

Masculine Singular	מֶלֶךְ טוֹב	a good king
Feminine Singular	מַלְכָּה טוֹבָה	a good queen
Masculine Plural	מְלָכִים טוֹבִים	good kings
Feminine Plural	מְלָכוֹת טוֹבוֹת	good queens

But what about masculine nouns that have feminine plural endings, such as אָבוֹת (fathers)? In such cases masculine adjectives must have the normal masculine plural ending (יםXX). Similarly, feminine adjectives must have the normal feminine plural ending (וֹת). Thus 'good fathers' is אָבוֹת טוֹבִים. And 'good cities' is עָרִים טוֹבוֹת.

It should also be noted that adjectives must also have הַ put in front of them plus a dot in the first letter if they describe definite nouns. Here are some examples:

Masculine Singular	הַמֶּלֶךְ הַטוֹב	the good king
Feminine Singular	הַמַּלְכָּה הַטוֹבָה	the good queen
Masculine Plural	הַמְּלָכִים הַטוֹבִים	the good kings
Feminine Plural	הַמְּלָכוֹת הַטוֹבוֹת	the good queens

The rules then for adjectives are simple: they always follow the pattern:

Masculine Singular	XXX
Feminine Singular	XXXָה
Masculine Plural	XXXִים
Feminine Plural	XXXוֹת

Adjectives

Remember: adjectives follow the nouns they describe and agree with them in terms of number, gender and definiteness.

You are now in a position to learn your first Hebrew sentences! Unlike English, Hebrew contains sentences without verbs. The simplest kind of sentence is composed simply of a noun and an adjective where 'is' is understood. The noun must be definite, and the adjective must be indefinite. For example, the sentence 'The man is good' is: הָאִישׁ טוֹב. Here the noun אִישׁ (man) is definite: הָאִישׁ. But the adjective that describes it is indefinite: טוֹב. As you can see, the verb 'is' is omitted. Here are some other examples:

הָאֵם טוֹבָה	The mother is good.
הָאִישׁ חָכָם	The man is wise.
הָאִשָּׁה זְקֵנָה	The woman is old.
הַבָּנִים חֲכָמִים	The sons are wise.

It is also possible to reverse the order of the adjectives and the nouns in such sentences. Thus there are two ways of saying 'The mother is good'. It can be either: הָאֵם טוֹבָה or טוֹבָה הָאֵם.

You should be careful then to distinguish between simple phrases where adjectives describe nouns and sentences where an adjective and noun are used. Thus:

בַּיִת גָּדוֹל	a big house
הַבַּיִת הַגָּדוֹל	the big house
הַבַּיִת גָּדוֹל	the house is big

Exercise 1

Translate the following:

אָב חָכָם	.1	אָבוֹת טוֹבִים	.10
מֶלֶךְ טוֹב	.2	אָב טוֹב	.11
עַם גָּדוֹל	.3	הַבַּיִת הַגָּדוֹל	.12
בֵּן טוֹב	.4	הַמִּשְׁפָּחָה הַטּוֹבָה	.13
בָּנִים טוֹבִים	.5	הָאָב הֶחָכָם	.14
בָּנוֹת טוֹבוֹת	.6	הַבָּתִּים הַגְּדוֹלִים	.15
דְּבָרִים טוֹבִים	.7	הַמִּשְׁפָּחוֹת הַטּוֹבוֹת	.16
מִשְׁפָּחוֹת טוֹבוֹת	.8	הָאָבוֹת הַחֲכָמִים	.17
עָרִים גְּדוֹלוֹת	.9		

Exercise 2

Translate the following:

הָעִיר גְּדוֹלָה	1.		הָאָרֶץ טוֹבָה	6.
הָאֵם טוֹבָה	2.		הָעָם גָּדוֹל	7.
הָאִישׁ זָקֵן	3.		הָאָב טוֹב	8.
הַבַּיִת גָּדוֹל	4.		הַסּוּס גָּדוֹל	9.
הָאִשָּׁה זְקֵנָה	5.		הַבָּנִים טוֹבִים	10.

CHAPTER NINE

Pronouns

Pronouns take the place of nouns. Let us look first at subject pronouns. In English the same pronoun can designate a masculine, feminine, singular or plural subject. The pronoun 'you' for example, can refer to one or more persons of either gender. Hebrew, however, has many more pronouns. Here is a list:

Subject Pronouns

I (m and f)	אֲנִי	we (m and f)	אֲנַחְנוּ
you (ms)	אַתָּה	you (mpl)	אַתֶּם
you (fs)	אַתְּ	you (fpl)	אַתֶּן
he	הוּא	they (m)	הֵם
she	הִיא	they (f)	הֵנָּה

These pronouns function in the same way as the nouns they replace. Here are some examples:

אֲנִי טוֹב	I am good	אֲנַחְנוּ טוֹבִים	we are good
אַתָּה טוֹב	you are good	אַתֶּם טוֹבִים	you are good
אַתְּ טוֹבָה	you are good	אַתֶּן טוֹבוֹת	you are good
הוּא טוֹב	he is good	הֵם טוֹבִים	they are good
הִיא טוֹבָה	she is good	הֵנָּה טוֹבוֹת	they are good

You might wonder what pronouns designate 'you' and 'they' when referring to groups of both men and women. In such cases the masculine plurals אַתֶּם (you) and הֵם (they) are used.

Like English, Hebrew also contains pronouns which are the objects of prepositions (such as 'to me') and verbs (such as 'the king kept him'). However, in Hebrew these object pronouns are attached to the prepositions and verbs. This is the general pattern:

Object Pronouns

Xִי or Xִנִי	me (m and f)	Xָנוּ	us (m and f)
Xְךָ	you (ms)	Xְכֶם	you (mpl)
Xֵךְ	you (fs)	Xְכֶן	you (fpl)
Xוֹ	him	Xְהֶם	them (m)
Xָהּ	her	Xְהֶן	them (f)

33

Here is an example using ל (to):

לִי	to me	לָנוּ	to us (m and f)
לְךָ	to you (ms)	לָכֶם	to you (mpl)
לָךְ	to you (fs)	לָכֶן	to you (fpl)
לוֹ	to him	לָהֶם	to them (m)
לָהּ	to her	לָהֶן	to them (f)

Here is an example using שָׁמַר (he kept):

שְׁמָרַנִי	he kept me	שְׁמָרָנוּ	he kept us (m and f)
שְׁמָרְךָ	he kept you (ms)		
שְׁמָרֵךְ	he kept you (fs)		
שְׁמָרוֹ	he kept him	שְׁמָרָם	he kept them (m)
שְׁמָרָהּ	he kept her	שְׁמָרָן	he kept them (f)

In addition to subject and object pronouns, there are several question pronouns. The first is the letter הֲ which is placed at the beginning of a sentence. For example, לֹא שָׁמַרְתָּ means 'you have not kept'. To turn this into a question the letter הֲ is placed at the beginning of the sentence: הֲלֹא שָׁמַרְתָּ. This means 'Have you not kept?' Other question pronouns are מִי (who?) and מָה (what?).

Another important pronoun is the substitution or relative pronoun אֲשֶׁר (which, where or who), as in הַמָּקוֹם אֲשֶׁר יָשַׁב (the place where he dwelt).

Exercise 1

Translate the following:

אֲנִי הָאִישׁ	1.	אֲנַחְנוּ הַבָּנִים	6.
אַתְּ הַבַּת	2.	הֵם אַחִים	7.
הוּא אִישׁ טוֹב	3.	הֵנָּה הַבָּנוֹת	8.
הוּא הַמָּקוֹם	4.	אֲנִי הַכֹּהֵן	9.
אַתָּה הָאִישׁ	5.	אַתְּ הַמַּלְכָּה	10.

Exercise 2

Using ל (to) and שָׁמַר (he kept):

.1	לִי		.5	לָהּ
.2	לָכֶם		.6	שְׁמָרָן
.3	לָהֶן		.7	שְׁמָרָהּ
.4	לָנוּ		.8	שְׁמָרֵךְ

Exercise 3

Translate the following:

1.   אֲנִי יְהוָה (Isa. 42.8)
2.   הִיא הָעִיר הַגְּדוֹלָה (Gen. 10.12)

CHAPTER TEN

Possessives

In English, possessives (such as my, your, etc.) precede the nouns they describe (such as '*my* house'). Hebrew, however, has many more possessives than English. And, unlike possessives in English, they are attached to ends of the nouns they refer to. There are two patterns of possessives depending on whether they are attached to singular or plural nouns. Here is the list of possessives added to singular nouns:

Possessive Adjectives for Singular Nouns

־ִי	my (m and f)	־ֵנוּ	our (m and f)
־ְךָ	your (ms)	־ְכֶם	your (mpl)
־ֵךְ	your (fs)	־ְכֶן	your (fpl)
־וֹ	his	־ָם	their (m)
־ָהּ	her	־ָן	their (f)

Where these forms are attached to singular nouns, there is no change in the noun, but when they are attached to feminine nouns ending in ־ָה the Hey (ה) becomes a Tav (ת) and there are often changes to the vowels.

Here are some examples:

סוּס horse (m)

סוּסִי	my (m and f) horse	סוּסֵנוּ	our (m and f) horse
סוּסְךָ	your (ms) horse	סוּסְכֶם	your (mpl) horse
סוּסֵךְ	your (fs) horse	סוּסְכֶן	your (fpl) horse
סוּסוֹ	his horse	סוּסָם	their (m) horse
סוּסָהּ	her horse	סוּסָן	their (f) horse

תּוֹרָה law (f)

תּוֹרָתִי	my (m and f) law	תּוֹרָתֵנוּ	our (m and f) law
תּוֹרָתְךָ	your (ms) law	תּוֹרַתְכֶם	your (mpl) law
תּוֹרָתֵךְ	your (fs) law	תּוֹרַתְכֶן	your (fpl) law
תּוֹרָתוֹ	his law	תּוֹרָתָם	their (m) law
תּוֹרָתָהּ	her law	תּוֹרָתָן	their (f) law

36

Possessives

These pronouns are attached to singular nouns, but a different pattern is used for plural nouns:

Possessive Adjectives for Plural Nouns

־ַי	my (m and f)	־ֵינוּ	our (m and f)
־ֶיךָ	your (ms)	־ֵיכֶם	your (mpl)
־ַיִךְ	your (fs)	־ֵיכֶן	your (fpl)
־ָיו	his	־ֵיהֶם	their (m)
־ֶיהָ	her	־ֵיהֶן	their (f)

When these possessive pronouns are added to plural masculine nouns, the masculine ending (־ִים) is dropped: thus סוּסִים (horses) becomes סוּסַי (my horses). Feminine plural nouns ending in וֹת, however, do not undergo any change.

Here are some examples:

סוּסִים horses (m)

סוּסַי	my (m and f) horses	סוּסֵינוּ	our (m and f) horses
סוּסֶיךָ	your (ms) horses	סוּסֵיכֶם	your (mpl) horses
סוּסַיִךְ	your (fs) horses	סוּסֵיכֶן	your (fpl) horses
סוּסָיו	his horses	סוּסֵיהֶם	their (m) horses
סוּסֶיהָ	her horses	סוּסֵיהֶן	their (f) horses

תּוֹרוֹת laws (f)

תּוֹרוֹתַי	my (m and f) laws	תּוֹרוֹתֵינוּ	our (m and f) laws
תּוֹרוֹתֶיךָ	your (ms) laws	תּוֹרוֹתֵיכֶם	your (mpl) laws
תּוֹרוֹתַיִךְ	your (fs) laws	תּוֹרוֹתֵיכֶן	your (fpl) laws
תּוֹרוֹתָיו	his laws	תּוֹרוֹתֵיהֶם	their (m) laws
תּוֹרוֹתֶיהָ	her laws	תּוֹרוֹתֵיהֶן	their (f) laws

Exercise 1

Translate the following:

11.	סוּסַיִךְ	1.	סוּסִי
12.	סוּסָיו	2.	סוּסָם
13.	סוּסֵיכֶם	3.	סוּסָן
14.	סוּסֵיהֶן	4.	תּוֹרָתֶךָ
15.	תּוֹרוֹתַי	5.	תּוֹרָתָן
16.	תּוֹרוֹתָיו	6.	תּוֹרָתֵנוּ
17.	תּוֹרוֹתֵינוּ	7.	תּוֹרָתוֹ
18.	תּוֹרוֹתֵיכֶן	8.	תּוֹרַתְכֶם
19.	תּוֹרוֹתֵיהֶן	9.	תּוֹרָתָהּ
20.	תּוֹרוֹתֵיהֶם	10.	סוּסִי

CHAPTER ELEVEN

Pointing Pronouns and Adjectives; The Linking Word

Pointing Pronouns

We now need to look at a special kind of pronoun. 'Pointing pronouns' (this, that, these, those) function the same way as other pronouns. Here is a list:

Pointing Pronouns

זֶה	this (m)	הוּא	that (m)
זֹאת	this (f)	הִיא	that (f)
אֵלֶּה	these (m and f)	הֵם	those (m)
		הֵן	those (f)

Here are some sentences using 'pointing pronouns':

זֶה אִישׁ	This is a man.
זֹאת אִשָּׁה	This is a woman.
אֵלֶּה סְפָרִים	These are books.
אֵלֶּה מִצְוֹת	These are commandments.
הוּא אִישׁ	That is a man.
הִיא אִשָּׁה	That is a woman.
הֵם סְפָרִים	Those are books.
הֵן מִצְוֹת	Those are commandments.

Pointing Adjectives

Similar forms are used for 'pointing adjectives' which are placed after the nouns they describe in the same way as ordinary adjectives. Note that because 'pointing adjectives' are definite they are used with definite nouns. Here is a list of the 'pointing adjectives':

Pointing Adjectives

הַזֶּה	this (m)	הַהוּא	that (m)
הַזֹּאת	this (f)	הַהִיא	that (f)
הָאֵלֶּה	these (m and f)	הָהֵם	those (m)
		הָהֵן	those (f)

Here are some examples:

הָאִישׁ הַזֶּה	this man
הָאִשָּׁה הַזֹּאת	this woman
הָאֲנָשִׁים הָאֵלֶּה	these men
הַנָּשִׁים הָאֵלֶּה	these women
הָאִישׁ הַהוּא	that man
הָאִשָּׁה הַהִיא	that woman
הָאֲנָשִׁים הָהֵם	those men
הַנָּשִׁים הָהֵן	those women

The Linking Word

Like English, Hebrew contains the linking word 'and', which is represented by the Vav (וֹ). Usually it has a Sheva (X) and is attached to the word which follows it. Here are some examples:

וְאָדָם	and a man
וְסוּס	and a horse
וְהָאָדָם	and the man

However, depending on the words which follow the Vav, the Sheva (X) can be replaced by other vowels. When, for example, the Vav is linked to a word whose first letter has a Sheva, as in שְׁמוּאֵל (Samuel), the Vav takes a dot (וּ). This happens because of the rhythm of speech. Thus 'and Samuel' is וּשְׁמוּאֵל (rather than וְשְׁמוּאֵל). Similarly, if the Vav precedes words beginning with מ, ב, פ it also takes the form וּ. Here are some examples:

וּבַת	and a daughter
וּמֹשֶׁה	and Moses
וּפֹה	and here

If the Vav precedes a word beginning with יְ, as in יְהוּדָה (Judah), something special takes place: the Sheva becomes a Hireq (X). Thus 'and Judah' becomes וִיהוּדָה. Here the Yod (י) is joined with the Hireq (X) which precedes it and together they are pronounced as an Open Hireq (יX).

Another change takes place if the Vav precedes a Hataf Qames (X), Hataf Patah (X) or Hataf Segol (X). In such cases, וֹ is replaced by either וַ, וָ or וֶ depending on which of these Hataf vowels follows the

Vav. Here are some examples:

וַאֲנִי and I

וֶאֱדוֹם and Edom

Finally, if the Vav is placed before a stressed syllable it becomes וָ, as in יוֹם וָלַיְלָה (day and night).

You should note that in general the Vav means 'and'; however, the same word can also mean 'but' or 'or' depending on the context. Thus וְסוּס usually means 'and a horse', but it can also mean 'but a horse', or 'or a horse'.

Exercise 1

Translate the following:

6. זֹאת הָעִיר הַטּוֹבָה		1. זֶה הַיּוֹם	
7. הִיא הַבְּרִית הַטּוֹבָה		2. זֹאת הַתּוֹרָה	
8. זֹאת הַבְּרָכָה		3. קָדוֹשׁ הַמָּקוֹם הַזֶּה	
9. זֶה סוּסֵנוּ		4. טוֹבִים הַדְּבָרִים הָאֵלֶּה	
		5. זֶה הָעָם	

Exercise 2

Translate the following:

5. וְהַסּוּסִים		1. וְסוּס	
6. וְהָאוֹר		2. וְהַכֶּסֶף	
7. וּמֶלֶךְ		3. וּדְבָרִים	
8. וְגַם		4. וְהָאָדָם	

Exercise 3

Translate the following:

אֵלֶּה הַדְּבָרִים אֲשֶׁר (which) תַּעֲשׂוּ (you shall do) בַּיּוֹם הַהוּא (Zech. 8.16)

CHAPTER TWELVE

Prepositions

As we saw in the chapter about pronouns, prepositions can be attached to object pronouns such as לִי (to me), לוֹ (to him), לָהֶם (to them). What about prepositions before nouns? As in English, many prepositions stand as separate words before nouns such as בֵּין (between), מוּל (opposite), לִפְנֵי (before). Here are some examples.

בֵּין הָעֵצִים   between the trees
מוּל הַמֶּלֶךְ   opposite the king
לִפְנֵי הַבַּיִת   before the house

However, just as Hebrew prepositions can be attached to pronouns, so they can also be attached to nouns. In such cases a Sheva (X) is placed under the preposition. Thus 'to Moses' is לְמֹשֶׁה. Here are some other examples.

לְעֵשָׂו   to Esau
בְּמֶלֶךְ   in a king
כְּאָדָם   like a man

If a preposition is attached to a noun whose first letter has a Sheva (such as שְׁמוּאֵל), the Sheva is replaced by a Hireq (X). Thus 'to Samuel' is לִשְׁמוּאֵל (rather than לְשְׁמוּאֵל). Here are other examples:

לִמְלָכִים   to kings
בִּמְלָכִים   in kings
כִּמְלָכִים   like kings

An exception to this rule occurs when prepositions are attached to nouns beginning יְ (such as יְהוּדָה). Here the Sheva disappears and יְ is linked to the Hireq (X) under the preposition which precedes it. Together they are pronounced 'ee'. Thus 'to Judah' becomes לִיהוּדָה (rather than לְיהוּדָה). These are other examples:

לִירוּשָׁלַיִם   to Jerusalem
בִּירוּשָׁלַיִם   in Jerusalem
כִּירוּשָׁלַיִם   like Jerusalem

42

Another special case occurs when a preposition is attached to a noun whose first letter has a Hataf vowel, such as אֲרִי (lion). Here the preposition takes the same vowel as the Hataf vowel. Thus 'to a lion' is לַאֲרִי. These are other examples:

לֶאֱדוֹם to Edom
בֶּאֱדוֹם in Edom
כֶּאֱדוֹם like Edom

So far we have looked at prepositions that are attached to indefinite nouns. What happens when they are linked to definite nouns (such as הַמֶּלֶךְ)? In such cases the ה disappears and its vowel is placed under the preposition. Thus 'to the king' is לַמֶּלֶךְ (rather than לְהַמֶּלֶךְ). Here is another example:

לָאָדָם to the man (rather than לְהָאָדָם)

Another preposition מִן (from) is usually attached to a noun. In this case the Nun (נ) disappears and a dot is placed in the first letter of the noun. Thus 'from Saul' is מִשָּׁאוּל. These are some other examples:

מִמֶּלֶךְ from a king
מִיּוֹם from a day
מִלַּיְלָה from a night

Before א, ה, ח, ר however the Hireq (X) is replaced by a Sere (X): thus 'from a man' is מֵאָדָם. Here are some other examples:

מֵעִיר from a city
מֵחשֶׁךְ from darkness
מֵראשׁ from a head

When מִן is attached to a definite noun (such as הַמֶּלֶךְ), הַ is not eliminated: thus 'from the king' is מֵהַמֶּלֶךְ.

Exercise 1

Translate the following:

.10	כַּמֶּלֶךְ	.1	בְּמִשְׁפָּחָה
.11	בַּדֶּרֶךְ	.2	כְּמֶלֶךְ
.12	בָּהָר	.3	לְמוֹאָב
.13	בָּאָרֶץ	.4	לְאָח
.14	לַמֶּלֶךְ	.5	כִּמְלָכִים
.15	לְאָדָם	.6	לִירוּשָׁלַיִם
.16	בְּחֹדֶשׁ	.7	בַּבַּיִת
.17	לִשְׁמוּאֵל	.8	לָעִיר
.18	לֶאֱדוֹם	.9	בְּבַיִת

Exercise 2

Translate the following:

.4	מֵאָדָם	.1	מִבַּיִת
.5	מִשְׁמוּאֵל	.2	מֵאִישׁ
		.3	מֵהַמֶּלֶךְ

44

CHAPTER THIRTEEN

Word Pairs

In English, nouns can be linked together by using the preposition 'of'. Here are a few examples: 'a man of peace', 'a man of valour', 'a time of war'. Unlike English, Hebrew nouns can be joined together without using a linking word. The first noun of such a Word Pair (known also as a construct) should be translated with 'of' following it as in:

מֶלֶךְ שָׁלוֹם   a king of peace

In many cases the vowels in the first noun in a Word Pair undergo a change, as in the following:

בֵּית עֲבָדִים   a house of slaves
(rather than בַּיִת עֲבָדִים)
דְּבַר מֶלֶךְ   a word of a king
(rather than דָּבָר מֶלֶךְ)

If the first word of a Word Pair ends in Hey (ה) it changes into a Tav (ת). Here are some examples:

מִשְׁפַּחַת אַחִים   a family of brothers
(rather than מִשְׁפָּחָה אַחִים)
בֶּהֱמַת שָׂדֶה   a beast of the field
(rather than בְּהֵמָה שָׂדֶה)

So far we have looked at indefinite Word Pairs. What about Word Pairs that are definite? In such cases the first noun of the Word Pair is indefinite, but the second noun is definite. The entire Word Pair thereby becomes definite. Here are some examples:

אֶרֶץ הָעָם   the land of the people
בֶּן הַמֶּלֶךְ   the son of the king
בַּת דָּוִד   the daughter of David

In some situations it is possible to join together several words to make Word Strings. For example, דְּבַר אֵשֶׁת מֶלֶךְ (a word of a wife of a king) consists of three nouns linked together. The first two nouns have undergone changes in their vowels and consonants (דָּבָר has become דְּבַר and אִשָּׁה has become אֵשֶׁת). This is an indefinite Word String; a Word String becomes definite if the last noun is definite, as in דְּבַר אֵשֶׁת הַמֶּלֶךְ (the word of the wife of the king).

In nouns ending in ים, the Mem (ם) disappears and the Hireq (ִי) is replaced by a Sere (ֵי). Thus 'horses of a king' is סוּסֵי מֶלֶךְ (rather than סוּסִים מֶלֶךְ). These are other examples:

בְּנֵי מֶלֶךְ sons of a king

דִּבְרֵי הַמֶּלֶךְ the words of the king

Just as prepositions can be attached to nouns, so they can also be attached to Word Pairs. Here are some examples:

בְּעֵינֵי הַמֶּלֶךְ in the eyes of the king

לְאַנְשֵׁי הַמֶּלֶךְ to the men of the king

You should note that when adjectives describe Word Pairs they follow the Word Pair and agree in definiteness and with the gender and number of the first noun. Here are some examples:

סוּס מֶלֶךְ טוֹב a good horse of a king

סוּסֵי הַמֶּלֶךְ טוֹבִים the good horses of the king

Similarly, if a Word Pair is the subject of a sentence, the verb must agree with the first noun of the Word Pair, as in:

בֶּן הַמַּלְכָּה זָכַר the son of the queen remembered.

Exercise 1

Translate the following:

.11	אֲדוֹן הַכֹּל	.1	דְּבַר מֶלֶךְ
.12	אֵשֶׁת אַבְרָהָם	.2	אֵשֶׁת מֶלֶךְ
.13	מֶלֶךְ מִצְרַיִם	.3	מֶלֶךְ שָׁלוֹם
.14	בַּת דָּוִד	.4	אִישׁ מִלְחָמָה
.15	דֶּרֶךְ הַמֶּלֶךְ	.5	אֵשֶׁת אִישׁ
.16	עִיר שָׁלוֹם	.6	אִישׁ הָהָר
.17	רֹאשׁ הַנַּעַר	.7	יוֹם שָׁלוֹם
.18	לֵב הָאִישׁ	.8	קוֹל הַבֵּן
.19	יַד מֹשֶׁה	.9	בֶּן הַמֶּלֶךְ
.20	כֹּל הַיּוֹם	.10	דְּבַר שָׁלוֹם

Exercise 2

Translate the following:

דְּבַר אֵשֶׁת מֶלֶךְ	.1		מִיַּד מֹשֶׁה	6.
רֹאשׁ עִיר מֹשֶׁה	2.		אַנְשֵׁי הַמָּקוֹם	7.
שֵׁם בֶּן מֹשֶׁה	3.		עֵינֵי אָדָם	8.
לֵב אֵשֶׁת דָּוִד	4.		עֵינֵי הַמֶּלֶךְ	9.
לְהַר הַמִּדְבָּר	5.		בְּנֵי הָעִיר	10.

Exercise 3

Translate the following:

1. בָּנִיתָ (you have built) אֶת בֵּית יְהוָה וְאֶת בֵּית הַמֶּלֶךְ (1 Kings 9.1)

2. טוֹב דְּבַר יְהוָה (2 Kings 20.19)

CHAPTER FOURTEEN

Numbers; Existence; Comparison

In Hebrew, numbers are represented by Hebrew letters. The following is a table of the numerical value of each letter.

Hebrew Letter	Numerical Value	Hebrew Letter	Numerical Value
א	1	ל	30
ב	2	מ	40
ג	3	נ	50
ד	4	ס	60
ה	5	ע	70
ו	6	פ	80
ז	7	צ	90
ח	8	ק	100
ט	9	ר	200
י	10	ש	300
כ	20	ת	400

The larger numbers are written first – thus numbers are represented by combinations of these letters. For example: יא=11; כא=21; לב=32; קא=101; קיא=111; ריב=212; תקה=505; תר=600. There are two exceptions to this pattern: 15 is טו and 16 is טז since יה and יו represent the name of God.

Numbers in Hebrew can also be written out. Like English they can serve as adjectives following the nouns they modify. The adjectives are either masculine or feminine. Here are some examples:

בֵּן רִאשׁוֹן   a first son
בַּת רִאשׁוֹנָה   a first daughter

Generally, however, numbers in Hebrew function as nouns. Again, there are masculine and feminine forms of these numbers depending on what they refer to. Here is a list:

Number	Masculine	Feminine
1	אֶחָד	אַחַת
2	שְׁנַיִם	שְׁתַּיִם
3	שְׁלֹשָׁה	שָׁלֹשׁ
4	אַרְבָּעָה	אַרְבַּע
5	חֲמִשָּׁה	חָמֵשׁ
6	שִׁשָּׁה	שֵׁשׁ
7	שִׁבְעָה	שֶׁבַע
8	שְׁמֹנָה	שְׁמֹנֶה
9	תִּשְׁעָה	תֵּשַׁע
10	עֲשָׂרָה	עֶשֶׂר

When indicating the number of something such as 'two sons', the numbers can function as the first noun of a Word Pair. Thus 'two sons' is שְׁנֵי בָנִים where שְׁנֵי means 'two of' or 'a pair of'. When a number is the first noun of a Word Pair, it often undergoes changes in vowels and consonants. Thus here 'two' as the first noun of a Word Pair is שְׁנֵי rather than שְׁנַיִם. Here are some other examples:

שֵׁשֶׁת בָּנִים six sons
(rather than שִׁשָּׁה בָּנִים)
שְׁבַע בָּנוֹת seven daughters
(rather than שֶׁבַע בָּנוֹת)
תְּשַׁע בָּנוֹת nine daughters
(rather than תֵּשַׁע בָּנוֹת)

Finally, regarding numbers in Hebrew, it should be noted that some words have a special form indicating pairs of things. This is produced by adding ־יִם to the singular noun. Here is an example:

יָד hand (singular)   יָדַיִם hands (a pair)

In Hebrew there are several words that indicate whether something exists or does not exist. The word יֵשׁ means 'there is' or 'there are'. It does not need to agree with any other word in the sentence. Thus it can be used with either masculine or feminine, singular or plural nouns. Here are some examples:

יֵשׁ אִשָּׁה בַּשָּׂדֶה There is a woman in the field.
יֵשׁ מְלָכִים בַּשָּׂדֶה There are kings in the field.

The word אֵין means 'there is not' or 'there are not'. Here are some examples:

49

אֵין אִשָּׁה בַּשָּׂדֶה There is not a woman in the field.

אֵין מְלָכִים בַּשָּׂדֶה There are not kings in the field.

Unlike English, Hebrew does not have words for making comparisons like 'big', 'bigger', 'biggest'. Instead it is possible to compare one thing with another by using the preposition מִן. In these cases the preposition follows the adjective. Here are some examples:

דָּוִד גָּדוֹל מִשָּׁאוּל David is greater than Saul.

הַבַּיִת גָּדוֹל מִן הָאֹהֶל The house is bigger than the tent.

It is also possible in Hebrew to indicate that something is best. This can be expressed by adding הַ to an adjective which follows a definite noun – as in דָּוִד הַמֶּלֶךְ הַגָּדוֹל – this is then followed by מִן attached to the word with which הַמֶּלֶךְ is compared. Thus דָּוִד הַמֶּלֶךְ הַגָּדוֹל מִכֹּל הַמְּלָכִים (David is the greatest king of all of the kings). Here is another example:

הִיא הַמַּלְכָּה הַגְּדוֹלָה מִכֹּל She is the greatest queen of all the

הַמְּלָכוֹת queens.

Another way of expressing that something is best is to make an adjective the first word of a Word Pair. Thus: דָּוִד גְּדוֹל בָּנָיו (David is the greatest of his brothers).

Exercise 1

Write the number of each of the following:

.1	יא	.6	תתר
.2	לא	.7	ריד
.3	קא	.8	תק
.4	קכב	.9	יז
.5	רכג	.10	כח

Exercise 2

Translate the following:

.1	אִשָּׁה רִאשׁוֹנָה	.4	שְׁמֹנֶה בָּנוֹת
.2	הָאִישׁ הָרִאשׁוֹן	.5	שְׁמוּאֵל גָּדוֹל מִדָּוִד
.3	שְׁלֹשֶׁת הַבָּנִים		

CHAPTER FIFTEEN

The Verb; Continuous Action

Unlike English, Hebrew verbs consist of three consonants. Here are some examples:

נתן	give	ישב	sit
שמר	keep	למד	learn
הלך	go	כתב	write
עמד	stand	אמר	say

In English, verbs designate present, past or future action. Hebrew, however, is different: actions are either Continuous, Completed or Uncompleted.

In addition Hebrew also contains commands (such as 'go!', 'leave!') as well as infinitives (such as 'to go', 'to learn'). To indicate whether an action is Continuous, Completed or Uncompleted, changes are made to the vowels under the three consonants of the verb and certain letters are added at either the beginning or the end of the consonants. You will be glad to learn that these additions are generally the same for all verbs.

Hebrew verbs are of two types: regular and irregular. Regular verbs preserve the three consonants in all forms; irregular verbs, however, do not always preserve these consonants. Sometimes one or even two of them disappear! I shall tell you more about this later.

You will also be pleased to know that there is a close relationship between verbs and nouns in Hebrew. Frequently nouns related to verbs also contain the same three consonants.

Thus, for example, כתב are the three consonants of the verb 'write'; the noun מִכְתָּב (letter) similarly contains these consonants. This means that it is often easy to recognize the meaning of nouns if you know the verbs they relate to, and vice versa.

In English the verb generally follows the subject of the sentence, as in: 'The cat purred'. In Hebrew, verbs usually begin sentences (except verbs in the Continuous tense). Here are some examples:

הָלַךְ דָּוִד David walked

נָתַן שְׁמוּאֵל Samuel gave

שָׁמַר הַמֶּלֶךְ the king kept

Another difference between Hebrew and English is that whenever the verb has a direct object, the word אֶת is added before it. This word is not translated – it simply indicates that the verb has a direct object. Here is an example:

זָכַר הַמֶּלֶךְ אֶת הַבֵּן The king remembered the son.

Continuous Action

Let us look now at the verbal forms which indicate Continuous Action. In Hebrew, 'ing'-words such as 'keeping', 'sitting' (known as participles) are placed after nouns and pronouns to indicate that an action is in progress. In such cases 'is' is understood. Here are some examples:

הַמֶּלֶךְ יוֹשֵׁב the king is sitting

יוֹסֵף אוֹכֵל Joseph is eating

הוּא שׁוֹמֵר he is keeping

You will be glad to know that there are only four forms of these 'ing'-words:

| Masculine Singular | xxíx | Masculine Plural | xxíxים |
| Feminine Singular | txxíx | Feminine Plural | xíxxíx |

As you can see, these 'ing'-words are similar to adjectives and thus agree with the pronoun they describe. Here is an example of the 'ing'-word 'keeping' joined to subject pronouns:

אֲנִי שׁוֹמֵר I (m) am keeping

אֲנִי שׁוֹמֶרֶת I (f) am keeping

אַתָּה שׁוֹמֵר you (ms) are keeping

אַתְּ שׁוֹמֶרֶת you (fs) are keeping

הוּא שׁוֹמֵר he is keeping

הִיא שׁוֹמֶרֶת she is keeping

אֲנַחְנוּ שׁוֹמְרִים we (m) are keeping

אֲנַחְנוּ שׁוֹמְרוֹת we (f) are keeping

אַתֶּם שׁוֹמְרִים you (mpl) are keeping

אַתֶּן שׁוֹמְרוֹת you (fpl) are keeping

הֵם שׁוֹמְרִים they (m) are keeping

הֵנָה שׁוֹמְרוֹת they (f) are keeping

These same 'ing'-words can also be used as nouns. In these cases they stand by themselves. Thus for example שׁוֹמֵר means 'one who is keeping'; if הַ is attached (הַשּׁוֹמֵר), it becomes 'the one who is keeping'. Here are some other examples:

כּוֹתֵב one who is writing

הַכּוֹתֵב the one who is writing

These 'ing'-words can also be used to describe nouns. In such cases they follow the nouns and agree with them in number, gender and definiteness. Here are some examples:

אִישׁ יוֹשֵׁב a sitting man

מַלְכָּה יוֹשֶׁבֶת a sitting queen

הַמֶּלֶךְ הַיּוֹשֵׁב the sitting king

'Ing'-words can also be used to express Passive Continuous Action (known as passive participles). Such forms indicate that a person or thing is acted upon. Again there are only four forms:

Masculine Singular	XXוּX	Masculine Plural	XXוּXים
Feminine Singular	XXוּXה	Feminine Plural	XXוּXוֹת

Here is an example using the Passive Continuous form with the subject pronouns:

אֲנִי שָׁמוּר I (m) am being kept

אֲנִי שְׁמוּרָה I (f) am being kept

אַתָּה שָׁמוּר you (ms) are being kept

אַתְּ שְׁמוּרָה you (fs) are being kept

הוּא שָׁמוּר he is being kept

הִיא שְׁמוּרָה she is being kept

אֲנַחְנוּ שְׁמוּרִים we (m) are being kept

אֲנַחְנוּ שְׁמוּרוֹת we (f) are being kept

אַתֶּם שְׁמוּרִים you (mpl) are being kept

אַתֶּן שְׁמוּרוֹת you (fpl) are being kept

הֵם שְׁמוּרִים they (m) are being kept

הֵנָה שְׁמוּרוֹת they (f) are being kept

As with Continuous Action, passive 'ing'-words can also be used as nouns. In such cases, they stand by themselves as in הַכָּתוּב (the written one). Such 'ing'-words can also describe nouns, as in:

דָּבָר כָּתוּב a written word
הַדָּבָר הַכָּתוּב the written word

Exercise 1

Translate the following:

הוּא שׁוֹמֵר	1.	אַתָּה שׁוֹמֵר	5.
הֵם שׁוֹמְרִים	2.	אַתֶּם שׁוֹמְרִים	6.
הֵנָּה שׁוֹמְרוֹת	3.	אֲנִי שׁוֹמֶרֶת	7.
אַתְּ שׁוֹמֶרֶת	4.	אַתֶּן שׁוֹמְרוֹת	8.

Exercise 2

Translate the following:

הוּא שׁוֹמֵר	1.	הוּא כָּתוּב	4.
הַשׁוֹמֵר	2.	הַכָּתוּב	5.
הָאִישׁ הַשׁוֹמֵר	3.	הַדָּבָר הַכָּתוּב	6.

CHAPTER SIXTEEN

Completed Action;
Uncompleted Action

You will be pleased to know that Completed Actions in Hebrew
(known as the Perfect tense) are formed in a simple way: endings
are attached to the consonants of the verb. These endings are always
the same regardless of the verb. And to make matters simple, each
ending designates a specific person. Unlike English, each verb form
thus indicates the person doing the action. Here is a list:

תִּיXXX	I (m and f)	נוXXX	we (m and f)
תָּXXX	you (ms)	תֶּםXXX	you (mpl)
תְּXXX	you (fs)	תֶּןXXX	you (fpl)
XXX	he	וXXX	they (m and f)
הXXX	she		

The following is an example using שמר (keep):

שָׁמַרְתִּי I kept/have kept/had kept
שָׁמַרְתָּ you (ms) kept/have kept/had kept
שָׁמַרְתְּ you (fs) kept/have kept/had kept
שָׁמַר he kept/has kept/had kept
שָׁמְרָה she kept/has kept/had kept
שָׁמַרְנוּ we (m and f) kept/have kept/had kept
שְׁמַרְתֶּם you (mpl) kept/have kept/had kept
שְׁמַרְתֶּן you (fpl) kept/have kept/had kept
שָׁמְרוּ they (m and f) kept/have kept/had kept

Where the verb stands alone, the person completing the action is
understood; it is not necessary to add subject pronouns. But nouns
can be added to sentences to indicate who is doing the action. Here
are some examples (remember the verb comes before the noun):

הָלַךְ הַמֶּלֶךְ the king went
הָלְכוּ הַמְּלָכִים the kings went
יָשְׁבוּ הַנְּעָרִים the young men sat

55

Uncompleted Actions in Hebrew (known as the Imperfect tense) are also formed simply: here extra letters and vowels are added to the consonants, at the beginning and sometimes at both the beginning and the end. These additions indicate the person doing the action and they are the same for all verbs. Here is the pattern:

אxxx	I (m and f)	נxxx	we (m and f)
תxxx	you (ms)	תxxxו	you (mpl)
תxxxי	you (fs)	תxxxנָה	you (fpl)
יxxx	he	יxxxו	they (m)
תxxx	she	תxxxנָה	they (f)

Here is an example using שמר:

אֶשְׁמֹר	I (m and f) will keep	נִשְׁמֹר	we (m and f) will keep
תִּשְׁמֹר	you (ms) will keep	תִּשְׁמְרוּ	you (mpl) will keep
תִּשְׁמְרִי	you (fs) will keep	תִּשְׁמֹרְנָה	you (fpl) will keep
יִשְׁמֹר	he will keep	יִשְׁמְרוּ	they (m) will keep
תִּשְׁמֹר	she will keep	תִּשְׁמֹרְנָה	they (f) will keep

In Hebrew these Uncompleted Actions can be translated in various ways depending on the context; in all cases they indicate actions which are not completed (such as 'was keeping', 'used to keep', 'will be keeping').

Hebrew has a very odd convention. When the Vav (ו) is placed before the verb, it sometimes changes a Completed verb to an Uncompleted verb, or vice versa (an Uncompleted verb into a Completed verb). The rule is: (1) ו before a Completed verb may turn it into an Uncompleted verb. For example, וְשָׁמַר means either 'and he kept' or 'and he will keep'; (2) ו before an Uncompleted verb must turn it into a Completed verb. For example, וַיִּשְׁמֹר means 'and he kept'. Note that ו before an Uncompleted verb does not change the tense. In some cases the addition of a ו before the Uncompleted verb changes the spelling because the stress shifts. For example, 'he will sit' is וַיֵּשֶׁב rather than וַיֵּשֵׁב.

Another thing to remember is that Completed and Uncompleted actions can be negated by adding לֹא (not) before the verb, as in לֹא שָׁמַר מֹשֶׁה (Moses has not kept) and לֹא יִשְׁמֹר מֹשֶׁה (Moses will not keep).

Exercise 1

Translate the following:

.1	שָׁמַר	.6	הָלַכְתְּ
.2	שָׁמַרְתְּ	.7	הָלַךְ הַמֶּלֶךְ
.3	שָׁמְרוּ הַמְּלָכִים	.8	שָׁמְרָה הַמַּלְכָּה
.4	עָמַדְנוּ	.9	יְשַׁבְתֶּם
.5	יָשְׁבוּ מְלָכוֹת		

Exercise 2

Translate the following:

.1	אֶשְׁמֹר	.5	תִּשְׁמֹרְנָה הַבָּנוֹת
.2	תִּשְׁמְרִי	.6	יִשְׁמְרוּ הַמְּלָכִים
.3	יִשְׁמֹר הַמֶּלֶךְ	.7	וַיִּשְׁמֹר
.4	תִּשְׁמוֹר הַמַּלְכָּה	.8	וְשָׁמַר

CHAPTER SEVENTEEN

Commands; Infinitives; Simple Mood

Commands

Like English, Hebrew also contains Commands (known as imperatives) such as 'go!', 'walk!', etc. In all these cases, 'you' is understood. Thus 'go!' really means 'you go!' There are therefore only four Commands: they are used when addressing you (ms), you (fs), you (mpl), you (fpl). You will be glad to know that these Commands are derived from verbal forms that you have already learned: Commands in Hebrew are identical with Uncompleted Action 'you' forms except that the ת which is placed before the consonants is removed. Here is an example of the Uncompleted Action 'you' forms and the Commands that are derived from them, using שׁמר (to keep):

Commands		*Uncompleted Action*	
שְׁמוֹר	Keep! (you ms)	תִּשְׁמוֹר	you (ms) will keep
שִׁמְרִי	Keep! (you fs)	תִּשְׁמְרִי	you (fs) will keep
שִׁמְרוּ	Keep! (you mpl)	תִּשְׁמְרוּ	you (mpl) will keep
שְׁמֹרְנָה	Keep! (you fpl)	תִּשְׁמֹרְנָה	you (fpl) will keep

You should note that sometimes there are vowel changes which take place under the main letters when Uncompleted forms are used to produce Commands.

Infinitives

In Hebrew, Infinitives are of two types. The first is formed by adding the preposition ל (to) to the main letters of the verb. Thus 'to keep' is לִשְׁמֹר. Here are some other examples:

לִזְכֹּר to remember
לִמְלֹךְ to rule

In the second type of Infinitive other prepositions such as בּ (in), כּ (like) or מִן (from) are attached to the main letters of the verb. Thus

58

בְּשְׁמֹר means 'in keeping'. Here are some other examples:

כְּזְכֹּר as remembering

מִשְּׁמֹר from keeping

Like other kinds of verbal forms, Infinitives can take an object. These are some examples:

לִשְׁמֹר אֶת הַבַּיִת to keep the house

לִזְכֹּר אֶת הַתּוֹרָה to remember the Torah

בְּשְׁמֹר אֶת הַבַּיִת in keeping the house

כְּזְכֹּר אֶת הַתּוֹרָה as remembering the Torah

In Hebrew it is possible to attach possessives (like those placed at the ends of nouns and prepositions) to the second type of Infinitives. Thus בְּשְׁמֹר means 'in keeping', whereas בְּשָׁמְרֵנוּ means 'in *our* keeping'. When possessives are added to Infinitive forms, vowel changes often take place.

In addition to these two types of Infinitives, there is also a special form of the Infinitive which is used for emphasis. This Infinitive of emphasis follows the pattern XîXX and is usually placed before the verb. Thus שָׁמוֹר שָׁמַר means 'he indeed kept'.

You will be glad to know that we have now learned the main forms of the verb:

Continuous Action
Completed Action
Uncompleted Action
Commands
Infinitives

Moods

We now need to look briefly at the main moods of the Hebrew verb. There are seven types, and each can be formed from the three consonants of the verb.

1. *Simple* (known as Paal or Kal). The first mood is the simplest as when שמר means 'keep'.
2. *Passive Simple* (known as Niphal). Here the Simple Mood is made passive as when שמר means 'be kept'.

3. *Intensive* (known as Piel). This mood expresses an intensive mood of the verb such as when כבד means 'honour'.

4. *Passive Intensive* (known also as Pual). This mood of the verb is the passive of the intensive mood as when כבד means 'be honoured'.

5. *Causative* (known also as Hiphiel). The causative mood expresses an action which causes something to happen such as when מלך means 'causes to rule'.

6. *Passive Causative* (known also as Hophal). This mood is the passive of the causative as when מלך means 'be caused to reign'.

7. *Reflexive* (known also as Hithpael). Here the mood of the verb conveys an action which is reflexive in character as when קדש means 'sanctify oneself'.

Thus in Hebrew the three consonants of the verb can express these various moods. But it should be noted that not all verbs actually have seven moods: most have only a few. We shall now look at each of these moods in turn in the following chapters.

Simple Mood

The Simple Mood is the easiest: it follows the pattern of the tenses we have already surveyed. שמר (to keep) is a good example: here it is in all the forms of the Simple Mood:

Continuous Action

אֲנִי שׁוֹמֵר	I (m) am keeping
אֲנִי שׁוֹמֶרֶת	I (f) am keeping
אַתָּה שׁוֹמֵר	you (ms) are keeping
אַתְּ שׁוֹמֶרֶת	you (fs) are keeping
הוּא שׁוֹמֵר	he is keeping
הִיא שׁוֹמֶרֶת	she is keeping
אֲנַחְנוּ שׁוֹמְרִים	we (m) are keeping
אֲנַחְנוּ שׁוֹמְרוֹת	we (f) are keeping
אַתֶּם שׁוֹמְרִים	you (mpl) are keeping
אַתֶּן שׁוֹמְרוֹת	you (fpl) are keeping
הֵם שׁוֹמְרִים	they (m) are keeping
הֵנָּה שׁוֹמְרוֹת	they (f) are keeping

Completed Action

שָׁמַרְתִּי	I (m and f) kept
שָׁמַרְתָּ	you (ms) kept
שָׁמַרְתְּ	you (fs) kept
שָׁמַר	he kept
שָׁמְרָה	she kept
שָׁמַרְנוּ	we (m and f) kept
שְׁמַרְתֶּם	you (mpl) kept
שְׁמַרְתֶּן	you (fpl) kept
שָׁמְרוּ	they (m and f) kept

Uncompleted Action

אֶשְׁמֹר	I will keep
תִּשְׁמֹר	you (ms) will keep
תִּשְׁמְרִי	you (fs) will keep
יִשְׁמֹר	he will keep
תִּשְׁמֹר	she will keep
נִשְׁמֹר	we (m and f) will keep
תִּשְׁמְרוּ	you (mpl) will keep
תִּשְׁמֹרְנָה	you (fpl) will keep
יִשְׁמְרוּ	they (m) will keep
תִּשְׁמֹרְנָה	they (f) will keep

Commands

שְׁמֹר	Keep! (ms)
שִׁמְרִי	Keep! (fs)
שִׁמְרוּ	Keep! (mpl)
שְׁמֹרְנָה	Keep! (fpl)

Infinitive

לִשְׁמֹר	to keep
שָׁמוֹר	indeed keep

Exercise

Translate the following:

11.	שָׁמְרִי	1.	לִשְׁמֹר
12.	נִשְׁמֹר	2.	שָׁמַר
13.	תִּשְׁמְרִי	3.	אֶשְׁמֹר
14.	יִשְׁמֹר	4.	שָׁמְרוּ
15.	שְׁמַרְתֶּם	5.	תִּשְׁמְרוּ
16.	הוּא שׁוֹמֵר	6.	תִּשְׁמֹרְנָה
17.	הֵם שׁוֹמְרִים	7.	שְׁמֹר
18.	שָׁמְרוּ	8.	שָׁמַרְתְּ
19.	הֵנָּה שׁוֹמְרוֹת	9.	שָׁמְרָה
20.	שָׁמַרְנוּ	10.	שְׁמֹרְנָה

CHAPTER EIGHTEEN

Passive Simple Mood

As mentioned in the last chapter, the Simple Mood of the verb has a
passive form (known also as Niphal): this expresses an action done
to the subject (like the Passive Continuous Action we previously
learned). Here are some other examples:

	Simple Mood	*Passive Simple Mood*
אמר	say	be said
בנה	build	be built
זכר	remember	be remembered
כרת	cut	be cut
נתן	give	be given

As you will see, the Passive Simple Mood is similar to the Simple
Mood but with various changes:

Continuous Action

Here a nun (נ) is placed at the beginning of the three consonants of
the verb and various vowel changes take place.

אֲנִי נִשְׁמָר	I (m) am being kept
אֲנִי נִשְׁמָרָה	I (f) am being kept
אַתָּה נִשְׁמָר	you (ms) are being kept
אַתְּ נִשְׁמָרָה	you (fs) are being kept
הוּא נִשְׁמָר	he is being kept
הִיא נִשְׁמָרָה	she is being kept
אֲנַחְנוּ נִשְׁמָרִים	we (m) are being kept
אֲנַחְנוּ נִשְׁמָרוֹת	we (f) are being kept
אַתֶּם נִשְׁמָרִים	you (mpl) are being kept
אַתֶּן נִשְׁמָרוֹת	you (fpl) are being kept
הֵם נִשְׁמָרִים	they (m) are being kept
הֵנָּה נִשְׁמָרוֹת	they (f) are being kept

Completed Action

Here נ is added to the three consonants of the verb. In addition, a number of different vowel changes take place.

נִשְׁמַרְתִּי I (m and f) was kept

נִשְׁמַרְתָּ you (ms) were kept

נִשְׁמַרְתְּ you (fs) were kept

נִשְׁמַר he was kept

נִשְׁמְרָה she was kept

נִשְׁמַרְנוּ we (m and f) were kept

נִשְׁמַרְתֶּם you (mpl) were kept

נִשְׁמַרְתֶּן you (fpl) were kept

נִשְׁמְרוּ they (m and f) were kept

Uncompleted Action

Here a dot is placed in the first consonant of the verb and again various vowel changes take place.

אֶשָּׁמֵר I (m and f) will be kept

תִּשָּׁמֵר you (ms) will be kept

תִּשָּׁמְרִי you (fs) will be kept

יִשָּׁמֵר he will be kept

תִּשָּׁמֵר she will be kept

נִשָּׁמֵר we (m and f) will be kept

תִּשָּׁמְרוּ you (mpl) will be kept

תִּשָּׁמַרְנָה you (fpl) will be kept

יִשָּׁמְרוּ they (m) will be kept

תִּשָּׁמַרְנָה they (f) will be kept

Commands

Here הִ is placed before the commands and a dot is put in the first consonant of the verb. Also, various vowel changes take place under the main letters.

הִשָּׁמֵר Be kept! (ms)

הִשָּׁמְרִי Be kept! (fs)

הִשָּׁמְרוּ Be kept! (mpl)

הִשָּׁמַרְנָה Be kept! (fpl)

64

Infinitive

In the Infinitive 'to be kept', הָ is placed before the consonants of the verb and a dot is placed in the first consonant:

לְהִשָּׁמֵר to be kept

In the emphatic Infinitive, נִ is placed before the three consonants of the verb:

נִשְׁמֹר indeed be kept

Here are some tips to help you recognize the Passive Simple Mood:

- נִ is placed before the three main letters of the verb in Continuous and Completed Actions.
- There is a dot in the first consonant of the verb in Uncompleted Actions.
- הָ is placed before three consonants of the verb and a dot is placed in the first consonant in Commands and the Infinitive.

NB. Through all this the personal endings and beginnings are the same as for the Simple Mood.

Exercise

Translate the following:

אֲנִי נִשְׁמָרָה	.1	תִּשָּׁמֵר	.11
הוּא נִשְׁמָר	.2	יִשָּׁמְרוּ	.12
אַתֶּם נִשְׁמָרִים	.3	הִשָּׁמַרְנָה	.13
הֵנָּה נִשְׁמָרוֹת	.4	הִשָּׁמֵר	.14
נִשְׁמַרְתִּי	.5	לְהִשָּׁמֵר	.15
נִשְׁמְרָה	.6	תִּשָּׁמְרוּ	.16
נִשְׁמַרְתֶּן	.7	הִשָּׁמְרִי	.17
נִשְׁמַרְתָּ	.8	אֲנַחְנוּ נִשְׁמָרוֹת	.18
אֶשָּׁמֵר	.9	נִשְׁמַרְתֶּם	.19
יִשָּׁמֵר	.10	הִיא נִשְׁמָרָה	.20

CHAPTER NINETEEN

Intensive Mood

The Intensive Mood (known also as Piel) indicates actions which are intensified or repeated. For example, שבר in the Simple Mood means 'break'. In the Intensive Mood it means 'shatter'. Here are some other examples:

	Simple Mood	Intensive Mood
שלח	send	send away
ספר	count	narrate

The following is the pattern of the Intensive Mood in its various forms.

Continuous Action

In Continuous Actions, מְ is placed before the three consonants of the verb and a dot is placed in the second consonant.

אֲנִי מְשַׁבֵּר	I (m) am shattering
אֲנִי מְשַׁבֶּרֶת	I (f) am shattering
אַתָּה מְשַׁבֵּר	you (ms) are shattering
אַתְּ מְשַׁבֶּרֶת	you (fs) are shattering
הוּא מְשַׁבֵּר	he is shattering
הִיא מְשַׁבֶּרֶת	she is shattering
אֲנַחְנוּ מְשַׁבְּרִים	we (m) are shattering
אֲנַחְנוּ מְשַׁבְּרוֹת	we (f) are shattering
אַתֶּם מְשַׁבְּרִים	you (mpl) are shattering
אַתֶּן מְשַׁבְּרוֹת	you (fpl) are shattering
הֵם מְשַׁבְּרִים	they (m) are shattering
הֵנָּה מְשַׁבְּרוֹת	they (f) are shattering

Completed Action

In Completed Actions there is a Hireq (X̣) under the first consonant of the verb, and a dot in the second consonant.

Intensive Mood

שִׁבַּרְתִּי I (m and f) shattered
שִׁבַּרְתָּ you (ms) shattered
שִׁבַּרְתְּ you (fs) shattered
שִׁבֵּר he shattered
שִׁבְּרָה she shattered
שִׁבַּרְנוּ we (m and f) shattered
שִׁבַּרְתֶּם you (mpl) shattered
שִׁבַּרְתֶּן you (fpl) shattered
שִׁבְּרוּ they (m and f) shattered

Uncompleted Action

In Uncompleted Actions there is a Sheva (x̧) under the letter added to the consonants of the verb (except א which takes a Hataf Patah (x̤)). In addition, a dot is placed in the second consonant.

אֲשַׁבֵּר I (m and f) will shatter
תְּשַׁבֵּר you (ms) will shatter
תְּשַׁבְּרִי you (fs) will shatter
יְשַׁבֵּר he will shatter
תְּשַׁבֵּר she will shatter
נְשַׁבֵּר we (m and f) will shatter
תְּשַׁבְּרוּ you (mpl) will shatter
תְּשַׁבֵּרְנָה you (fpl) will shatter
יְשַׁבְּרוּ they (m) will shatter
תְּשַׁבֵּרְנָה they (f) will shatter

Commands

Commands are formed in the usual way by dropping the letter that is placed before the three consonants of the verb in Uncompleted Actions.

שַׁבֵּר Shatter! (ms)
שַׁבְּרִי Shatter! (fs)
שַׁבְּרוּ Shatter! (mpl)
שַׁבֵּרְנָה Shatter! (fpl)

67

Infinitives

In the first type of Infinitive a Sheva (X̟) is placed under the preposition preceding the three consonants of the verb:

לְשַׁבֵּר to smash

The second type consists of the three main consonants with a dot in the second consonant:

שַׁבֵּר indeed smash

Here are some tips to help you recognize the Intensive Mood:

- There is a dot in the second consonant of the verb.
- In Continuing Actions the three consonants are preceded by מְ.
- In Completed Actions the first consonant has a Hireq (X̟).
- In Uncompleted Actions the letter placed before the three consonants of the verb has a Sheva (X̟) except א which has a Hataf Patah (X̟).
- Commands are formed in the usual way by dropping the letter that is placed before the Uncompleted 'you' forms.
- The Infinitive takes a Sheva (X̟) under the prepositions that precede it.

Exercise

Translate the following:

אֲנִי מְשַׁבֵּר	.1	נְשַׁבֵּר	.11
אֲנַחְנוּ מְשַׁבְּרִים	.2	יְשַׁבְּרוּ	.12
הִיא מְשַׁבֶּרֶת	.3	יְשַׁבֵּר	.13
הֵם מְשַׁבְּרִים	.4	שַׁבֵּר	.14
שִׁבַּרְתָּ	.5	שַׁבֵּרְנָה	.15
שִׁבַּרְנוּ	.6	לְשַׁבֵּר	.16
שִׁבַּרְתֶּם	.7	שַׁבְּרוּ	.17
שִׁבַּרְתְּ	.8	אַתָּה מְשַׁבֵּר	.18
אֲשַׁבֵּר	.9	שַׁבְּרוּ	.19
תְּשַׁבֵּר	.10		

CHAPTER TWENTY

Passive Intensive Mood

The Passive Intensive Mood (also known as Pual) is the Passive of the Intensive. Here are some examples:

	Intensive	*Passive Intensive*
שבר	shatter	be shattered
כבד	honour	be honoured
הלל	praise	be praised

The central characteristic of the Passive Intensive is a Qibbus (x̣) placed under the first consonant of the verb.

Continuous Action

As in the Intensive Form, מְ is placed before the three consonants of the verb and a dot is placed in the second consonant. Look out for the Qibbus under the first consonant.

אֲנִי מְשֻׁבָּר	I (m) am being shattered
אֲנִי מְשֻׁבֶּרֶת	I (f) am being shattered
אַתָּה מְשֻׁבָּר	you (ms) are being shattered
אַתְּ מְשֻׁבֶּרֶת	you (fs) are being shattered
הוּא מְשֻׁבָּר	he is being shattered
הִיא מְשֻׁבֶּרֶת	she is being shattered
אֲנַחְנוּ מְשֻׁבָּרִים	we (m) are being shattered
אֲנַחְנוּ מְשֻׁבָּרוֹת	we (f) are being shattered
אַתֶּם מְשֻׁבָּרִים	you (mpl) are being shattered
אַתֶּן מְשֻׁבָּרוֹת	you (fpl) are being shattered
הֵם מְשֻׁבָּרִים	they (m) are being shattered
הֵנָּה מְשֻׁבָּרוֹת	they (f) are being shattered

Completed Action

As with the Intensive Form there is a dot in the second consonant of the verb. Again, the Qibbus (ֻ) is placed under the first consonant.

שֻׁבַּרְתִּי I (m and f) was shattered
שֻׁבַּרְתָּ you (ms) were shattered
שֻׁבַּרְתְּ you (fs) were shattered
שֻׁבַּר he was shattered
שֻׁבְּרָה she was shattered
שֻׁבַּרְנוּ we (m and f) were shattered
שֻׁבַּרְתֶּם you (mpl) were shattered
שֻׁבַּרְתֶּן you (fpl) were shattered
שֻׁבְּרוּ they (m and f) were shattered

Uncompleted Action

As with the Intensive Mood a Sheva (ְ) is placed under the letter preceding the three consonants of the verb except א which takes a Hatef Patah (ֲ). Again, a Qibbus (ֻ) is placed under the first consonant, and a dot is placed in the second consonant.

אֲשֻׁבַּר I (m and f) will be shattered
תְּשֻׁבַּר you (ms) will be shattered
תְּשֻׁבְּרִי you (fs) will be shattered
יְשֻׁבַּר he will be shattered
תְּשֻׁבַּר she will be shattered
נְשֻׁבַּר we (m and f) will be shattered
תְּשֻׁבְּרוּ you (mpl) will be shattered
תְּשֻׁבַּרְנָה you (fpl) will be shattered
יְשֻׁבְּרוּ they (mpl) will be shattered
תְּשֻׁבַּרְנָה they (fpl) will be shattered

Commands

There are no Command forms.

Infinitive

There is no ordinary Infinitive.

שֻׁבֹּר indeed be shattered

70

Passive Intensive Mood

The Passive Intensive Mood is easily recognized: it follows the general pattern of the Intensive but has a Qibbus (ֻ) under the first consonant of the verb.

Exercise

Translate the following:

אַתָּה מְשֻׁבָּר	.1	תְּשֻׁבַּר	.11
אֲנַחְנוּ מְשֻׁבָּרִים	.2	יְשֻׁבַּר	.12
הֵנָּה מְשֻׁבָּרוֹת	.3	נְשֻׁבַּר	.13
הוּא מְשֻׁבָּר	.4	תְּשֻׁבַּרְנָה	.14
שֻׁבַּר	.5	יְשֻׁבְּרוּ	.15
שֻׁבַּרְתֶּם	.6	שֻׁבַּר	.16
שֻׁבַּרְתֶּן	.7	הִיא מְשֻׁבֶּרֶת	.17
שֻׁבְּרוּ	.8	אֲנַחְנוּ מְשֻׁבָּרוֹת	.18
שֻׁבַּרְנוּ	.9	אֲנִי מְשֻׁבֶּרֶת	.19
שֻׁבַּרְתִּי	.10	שֻׁבְּרָה	.20

CHAPTER TWENTY-ONE

Causative Mood

Verbs in the Causative Mood (known also as Hiphiel) express causative actions. Here are some examples:

	Simple Mood	*Causative Mood*
מלך	rule	cause to rule
עמד	stand	cause to stand
שמע	hear	cause to hear

The following is the pattern of the Causative Mood in its various forms.

Continuous Action

Here מַ precedes the three consonants of the verb. In addition, a Hireq (אִX) is placed between the second and third consonants in the masculine singular and masculine and feminine plural forms.

אֲנִי מַמְלִיךְ	I (m) am causing to rule
אֲנִי מַמְלֶכֶת	I (f) am causing to rule
אַתָּה מַמְלִיךְ	you (m) are causing to rule
אַתְּ מַמְלֶכֶת	you (f) are causing to rule
הוּא מַמְלִיךְ	he is causing to rule
הִיא מַמְלֶכֶת	she is causing to rule
אֲנַחְנוּ מַמְלִיכִים	we (m) are causing to rule
אֲנַחְנוּ מַמְלִיכוֹת	we (f) are causing to rule
אַתֶּם מַמְלִיכִים	you (m) are causing to rule
אַתֶּן מַמְלִיכוֹת	you (f) are causing to rule
הֵם מַמְלִיכִים	they (m) are causing to rule
הֵנָּה מַמְלִיכוֹת	they (f) are causing to rule

Completed Action

In Completed Actions, הִ is placed before the three consonants. In 'he', 'she' and 'they' forms there is a Hireq (אִX) between the second and third consonants.

הִמְלַכְתִּי	I (m and f) caused to rule
הִמְלַכְתָּ	you (ms) caused to rule
הִמְלַכְתְּ	you (fs) caused to rule
הִמְלִיךְ	he caused to rule
הִמְלִיכָה	she caused to rule
הִמְלַכְנוּ	we (m and f) caused to rule
הִמְלַכְתֶּם	you (mpl) caused to rule
הִמְלַכְתֶּן	you (fpl) caused to rule
הִמְלִיכוּ	they (m and f) caused to rule

Uncompleted Action

A Patah (X̱) is placed under the letter preceding the three consonants of the verb. In addition, there is a Hireq (יX̱) between the second and third consonants in all forms except 'you' and 'they' (fpl).

אַמְלִיךְ	I (m and s) will cause to rule
תַּמְלִיךְ	you (ms) will cause to rule
תַּמְלִיכִי	you (fs) will cause to rule
יַמְלִיךְ	he will cause to rule
תַּמְלִיךְ	she will cause to rule
נַמְלִיךְ	we (m and f) will cause to rule
תַּמְלִיכוּ	you (mpl) will cause to rule
תַּמְלֵכְנָה	you (fpl) will cause to rule
יַמְלִיכוּ	they (m) will cause to rule
תַּמְלֵכְנָה	they (f) will cause to rule

Commands

In commands, הַ is placed before all the forms.

הַמְלֵךְ	Cause to rule! (ms)
הַמְלִיכִי	Cause to rule! (fs)
הַמְלִיכוּ	Cause to rule! (mpl)
הַמְלֵכְנָה	Cause to rule! (fpl)

Infinitive

Here ה appears before the consonants of the verb.

לְהַמְלִיךְ to cause to rule

הַמְלֵךְ indeed cause to rule

These are some tips to help you identify the Causative Mood:

- מַ precedes the three consonants of the verb in Continuous Actions.
- הִ is placed before the three consonants of the verb in Completed Actions.
- A Patah (X̲) is placed under the consonant preceding the three consonants of the verb in Uncompleted Actions.
- הַ is placed before the three consonants in Commands and Infinitives.
- A Hireq ('X̲) is placed between the second and third consonants of the verb in many forms.

Exercise

Translate the following:

תַּמְלִיךְ	‎.11	אֲנִי מַמְלִיךְ	‎.1
נַמְלִיךְ	‎.12	הוּא מַמְלִיךְ	‎.2
תַּמְלֵכְנָה	‎.13	אֲנַחְנוּ מַמְלִיכִים	‎.3
תַּמְלִיכוּ	‎.14	הֵנָּה מַמְלִיכוֹת	‎.4
הַמְלִיכִי	‎.15	הִמְלַכְתְּ	‎.5
הַמְלִיכוּ	‎.16	הִמְלִיכָה	‎.6
הַמְלֵכְנָה	‎.17	הִמְלַכְתֶּם	‎.7
לְהַמְלִיךְ	‎.18	הִמְלִיכוּ	‎.8
הַמְלִיךְ	‎.19	אַמְלִיךְ	‎.9
הִמְלַכְנוּ	‎.20	תַּמְלִיכִי	‎.10

CHAPTER TWENTY-TWO

Passive Causative Mood

The Passive Causative Mood (known also as the Hophal) is the passive of the causative. Here are some examples:

	Causative	*Passive Causative*
גדל	cause to be great	be made great
מלך	cause to reign	be made to reign

The following is the pattern of the Passive Causative Mood.

Continuous Action

Here מָ is placed before the first three consonants of the verb.

אֲנִי מֻגְדָּל	I (m) am being made great
אֲנִי מֻגְדֶּלֶת	I (f) am being made great
אַתָּה מֻגְדָּל	you (ms) are being made great
אַתְּ מֻגְדֶּלֶת	you (fs) are being made great
הוּא מֻגְדָּל	he is being made great
הִיא מֻגְדֶּלֶת	she is being made great
אֲנַחְנוּ מֻגְדָּלִים	we (m) are being made great
אֲנַחְנוּ מֻגְדָּלוֹת	we (f) are being made great
אַתֶּם מֻגְדָּלִים	you (mpl) are being made great
אַתֶּן מֻגְדָּלוֹת	you (fpl) are being made great
הֵם מֻגְדָּלִים	they (m) are being made great
הֵנָּה מֻגְדָּלוֹת	they (f) are being made great

Completed Action

Here הָ is placed before the three consonants of the verb.

הָגְדַּלְתִּי	I (m and f) was made great
הָגְדַּלְתָּ	you (ms) were made great
הָגְדַּלְתְּ	you (fs) were made great
הָגְדַּל	he was made great
הָגְדְּלָה	she was made great

75

הִגְדַּלְנוּ we (m and f) were made great

הִגְדַּלְתֶּם you (mpl) were made great

הִגְדַּלְתֶּן you (fpl) were made great

הִגְדִּלוּ they (m and f) were made great

Uncompleted Action

In Uncompleted Actions, a Qames (x̱) is placed under the letter that precedes the three consonants of the verb.

אֻגְדַּל I (m and f) will be made great

תֻּגְדַּל you (ms) will be made great

תֻּגְדְּלִי you (fs) will be made great

יֻגְדַּל he will be made great

תֻּגְדַּל she will be made great

נֻגְדַּל we will be made great

תֻּגְדְּלוּ you (mpl) will be made great

תֻּגְדַּלְנָה you (fpl) will be made great

יֻגְדְּלוּ they (mpl) will be made great

תֻּגְדַּלְנָה they (fpl) will be made great

Commands

There are no Command forms.

Infinitive

Here הָ is placed before the three consonants of the verb.

הָגְדֵּל indeed be made great (emphatic infinitive)

Here are some tips for recognizing the Passive Causative:

- In Continuing Actions, מָ is placed before the three main consonants of the verb.
- In Completed Actions, הָ is placed before the three consonants of
  the verb.
- In Uncompleted Actions, a Qames (x̱) is placed before the three
  consonants of the verb.
- In the Infinitive, הָ is placed before the three consonants of the
  verb.

Exercise

Translate the following:

תֻּגְדַּל	11.		אֲנִי מָגְדָּל	1.
נֻגְדַּל	12.		אַתְּ מָגְדֶּלֶת	2.
תֻּגְדַּלְנָה	13.		אֲנַחְנוּ מָגְדָּלִים	3.
יֻגְדְּלוּ	14.		אַתֶּם מָגְדָּלִים	4.
הֻגְדַּל	15.		הֻגְדַּלְתְּ	5.
הוּא מָגְדָּל	16.		הֻגְדַּל	6.
הִיא מֻגְדֶּלֶת	17.		הֻגְדַּלְנוּ	7.
הֻגְדַּלְתְּ	18.		הֻגְדַּלְתֶּם	8.
הֻגְדְּלוּ	19.		הֻגְדְּלוּ	9.
			אֻגְדַּל	10.

Reflexive Mood

The Reflexive Mood (known also as Hithpael) expresses actions done to oneself. Here are some examples:

	Simple	*Reflexive*
הלל	praise	praise oneself
חזק	be strong	strengthen oneself
קדש	sanctify	sanctify oneself

The following is the pattern of the Reflexive Mood:

Continuous Action

Here מְת is placed before the three consonants of the verb. In addition a dot is placed in the second consonant.

אֲנִי מִתְקַדֵּשׁ I (m) am sanctifying myself
אֲנִי מִתְקַדֶּשֶׁת I (f) am sanctifying myself
אַתָּה מִתְקַדֵּשׁ you (ms) are sanctifying yourself
אַתְּ מִתְקַדֶּשֶׁת you (fs) are sanctifying yourself
הוּא מִתְקַדֵּשׁ he is sanctifying himself
הִיא מִתְקַדֶּשֶׁת she is sanctifying herself
אֲנַחְנוּ מִתְקַדְּשִׁים we (m) are sanctifying ourselves
אֲנַחְנוּ מִתְקַדְּשׁוֹת we (f) are sanctifying ourselves
אַתֶּם מִתְקַדְּשִׁים you (mpl) are sanctifying yourselves
אַתֶּן מִתְקַדְּשׁוֹת you (fpl) are sanctifying yourselves
הֵם מִתְקַדְּשִׁים they (m) are sanctifying themselves
הֵנָּה מִתְקַדְּשׁוֹת they (f) are sanctifying themselves

Completed Action

In Completed Actions, הְת is placed before the three consonants of the verb. Again, a dot is placed in the second consonant.

הִתְקַדַּשְׁתִּי I (m and f) sanctified myself
הִתְקַדַּשְׁתָּ you (ms) sanctified yourself

Reflexive Mood

הִתְקַדַּשְׁתְּ	you (fs) sanctified yourself
הִתְקַדֵּשׁ	he sanctified himself
הִתְקַדְּשָׁה	she sanctified herself
הִתְקַדַּשְׁנוּ	we (m and f) sanctified ourselves
הִתְקַדַּשְׁתֶּם	you (mpl) sanctified yourselves
הִתְקַדַּשְׁתֶּן	you (fpl) sanctified yourselves
הִתְקַדְּשׁוּ	they (m and f) sanctified themselves

Uncompleted Action

Here ת is placed after the normal consonants which precede the three consonants of the verb. In addition a dot is put in the second consonant.

אֶתְקַדֵּשׁ	I (m and f) will sanctify myself
תִּתְקַדֵּשׁ	you (ms) will sanctify yourself
תִּתְקַדְּשִׁי	you (fs) will sanctify yourself
יִתְקַדֵּשׁ	he will sanctify himself
תִּתְקַדֵּשׁ	she will sanctify herself
נִתְקַדֵּשׁ	we (m and f) will sanctify ourselves
תִּתְקַדְּשׁוּ	you (mpl) will sanctify yourselves
תִּתְקַדֵּשְׁנָה	you (fpl) will sanctify yourselves
יִתְקַדְּשׁוּ	they (m) will sanctify themselves
תִּתְקַדֵּשְׁנָה	they (f) will sanctify themselves

Commands

In Commands, הת is placed before the three consonants of the verb. In addition a dot is placed in the second consonant.

הִתְקַדֵּשׁ	Sanctify yourself! (ms)
הִתְקַדְּשִׁי	Sanctify yourself! (fs)
הִתְקַדְּשׁוּ	Sanctify yourselves! (mpl)
הִתְקַדֵּשְׁנָה	Sanctify yourselves! (fpl)

Infinitive

Here הת is placed before the three consonants of the verb. Again, a dot is placed in the second consonant.

לְהִתְקַדֵּשׁ to sanctify yourself

There is no emphatic Infinitive.

Here are some tips to recognize the Reflexive Mood:

- In Continuous Actions, מִת is placed before the three consonants of the verb and a dot is put in the second consonant.
- In Completed Actions, הִת is placed before the three consonants of the verb and a dot is put in the second consonant.
- In Uncompleted Actions a ת is placed after the letters that precede the three consonants of the verb. A dot is placed in the second consonant.
- In Commands, הִת is placed before the three consonants of the verb and a dot is put in the second consonant.
- In the Infinitive, הִת is placed before the three consonants of the verb and a dot is put in the second consonant.

Exercise

Translate the following:

הִתְקַדְּשׁוּ	9.		אֲנִי מִתְקַדֵּשׁ	1.
הִתְקַדֵּשׁ	10.		אַתָּה מִתְקַדֵּשׁ	2.
תִּתְקַדְּשִׁי	11.		הִיא מִתְקַדֶּשֶׁת	3.
יִתְקַדֵּשׁ	12.		אֲנַחְנוּ מִתְקַדְּשׁוֹת	4.
נִתְקַדֵּשׁ	13.		הֵנָּה מִתְקַדְּשׁוֹת	5.
תִּתְקַדֵּשְׁנָה	14.		הִתְקַדַּשְׁתָּ	6.
יִתְקַדְּשׁוּ	15.		הִתְקַדֵּשׁ	7.
			הִתְקַדַּשְׁתֶּם	8.

Irregular Verbs;
Using the Dictionary

Irregular Verbs

You have now learned all the Moods of the Verb: Simple (Paal), Simple Passive (Niphal), Intensive (Piel), Passive Intensive (Pual), Causative (Hiphiel), Passive Causative (Hophal) and Reflexive (Hithpael). These are the basic patterns of the regular verb. That is all there is to it! However, as I mentioned previously, Hebrew also contains irregular verbs. Unlike regular verbs, where the three consonants of the verb are stable, irregular verbs contain unstable consonants which affect these patterns. But even when this happens, the letters preceding and following the consonants remain the same.

In certain cases one or two of the three consonants drops out altogether. This can happen, for example, when such letters as א, ה, ו, ח, י, ע serve as the first, second or third consonants of the verb. To illustrate such alterations, here are two examples of Uncompleted Actions in the Simple Mood where the first consonant of the verb has disappeared:

	ידע (know)	הלך (go)
I (m and f)	אֵדַע	אֵלֵךְ
you (ms)	תֵּדַע	תֵּלֵךְ
you (fs)	תֵּדְעִי	תֵּלְכִי
he	יֵדַע	יֵלֵךְ
she	תֵּדַע	תֵּלֵךְ
we (m and f)	נֵדַע	נֵלֵךְ
you (mpl)	תֵּדְעוּ	תֵּלְכוּ
you (fpl)	תֵּדַעְנָה	תֵּלַכְנָה
they (m)	יֵדְעוּ	יֵלְכוּ
they (f)	תֵּדַעְנָה	תֵּלַכְנָה

In some cases the second consonant of the verb is dropped. Here are two examples of Completed Actions in the Simple Mood where this occurs:

	שִׂים (put)	בּוֹא (come)
I (m and f)	שַׂמְתִּי	בָּאתִי
you (ms)	שַׂמְתָּ	בָּאתָ
you (fs)	שַׂמְתְּ	בָּאת
he	שָׂם	בָּא
she	שָׂמָה	בָּאָה
we (m and f)	שַׂמְנוּ	בָּאנוּ
you (mpl)	שַׂמְתֶּם	בָּאתֶם
you (fpl)	שַׂמְתֶּן	בָּאתֶן
they (m and f)	שָׂמוּ	בָּאוּ

Using the Dictionary

Such changes in the patterns of the regular verb will make it difficult for you to recognize some verbs you will come across when reading the Bible. But help is at hand! You will be glad to know that there is a dictionary which analyses every verb (as well as every other word) in the Bible so that you will know both the main letters of the verb as well as its form: B. Davidson, *Analytic Hebrew and Chaldee Lexicon* (Hendrickson, New Edition 1990).

Let me explain how this dictionary works. You will remember that there are various kinds of Action in Hebrew. In addition there are Seven Moods of the verb. In this and other dictionaries all these terms have various abbreviations (listed in parentheses):

Actions
Continuous (part.)
Completed (perf. or pref.)
Uncompleted (imp. or fut.)
Command (imp.)
Infinitive (inf.)

Moods
Simple (Paal or Kal.)
Passive Simple (Niph.)
Intensive (Piel)
Passive Intensive (Pual)
Causative (Hiph.)
Passive Causative (Hoph.)
Reflexive (Hithpa.)

When you want to find the meaning of a verb, you need to do two things:

1. Look up the verb in the Davidson dictionary as it appears in the Bible to discover its constituent parts.
2. Look up the three consonants of the verb in the Davidson dictionary or a small dictionary to find its meaning. Be sure to look for the correct Mood, since the three consonants of the verb have different meanings in the various Moods.

Here are some examples of both regular and irregular verbs:

- You will find the verb שַׁלְחוּ analysed in the Davidson dictionary as: Piel. imp. pl. masc. שלח. This means that שַׁלְחוּ is a masculine plural Command in the Intensive Mood with שלח as its three consonants. You then need to look up שלח to find its basic meaning in the Intensive Mood (which is 'send'). Thus שַׁלְחוּ means 'Send!' (mpl).

- You will find the verb יִכְתֹּב analysed in the Davidson dictionary as: Kal. fut. 3 pers. sing. masc. כתב. This means that יִכְתֹּב is a 3rd person masculine singular Uncompleted Action in the Simple Mood with כתב as the three consonants of the verb. You then need to look up כתב in the Simple Mood (which means 'write'). יִכְתֹּב thus means 'he will write'.

- You will find the irregular verb אֹמַר analysed in the Davidson dictionary as: Kal. fut. 1 per. sing. אמר. This means that אֹמַר is a 1st person singular Uncompleted Action in the Simple Mood with אמר as the three consonants of the verb. In this irregular verb the first consonant has disappeared; the א is the consonant representing 'I' which is placed before the two remaining consonants (מר) of the verb. You then need to look up אמר in the Simple Mood (which means 'say'). Thus אֹמַר means 'I will say'.

As I mentioned, the Davidson dictionary analyses other kinds of words in the Bible in addition to verbs. Here is an example of the analysis of a noun:

You will find מַלְכּוֹ in the Davidson dictionary analysed as: Noun masc. sing. suff. 3 pers. sing. masc. מֶלֶךְ. This means that מַלְכּוֹ is a masculine singular noun with a 3 masculine singular suffix from מֶלֶךְ. Thus מַלְכּוֹ means 'his king'.

83

So there you are. You should be able to translate all words in the Bible using this Davidson dictionary. I should stress, however, that generally you will want to use a smaller dictionary. The Davidson dictionary is useful only when you are unable to analyse verbs or break down other kinds of words into their constitutive parts.

CHAPTER TWENTY-FIVE

Creation (Genesis 1.1–5)

Genesis 1.1

בְּרֵאשִׁית בָּרָא אֱלֹהִים אֵת הַשָּׁמַיִם וְאֵת הָאָרֶץ

The word בְּרֵאשִׁית (in the beginning) is composed of the preposition בּ (in) and the feminine singular noun רֵאשִׁית (beginning). The verb בָּרָא (he created) is 3rd person, Completed Action, Simple Mood, from ברא (create). The masculine singular noun אֱלֹהִים (God) is one of the names for God. אֵת indicates that the verb בָּרָא takes a definite object. הַשָּׁמַיִם (the heavens) is a masculine plural definite noun. אֵת is repeated to indicate that the verb בָּרָא takes another definite object. הָאָרֶץ (the earth) is a feminine singular definite noun.

In the beginning God created the heavens and the earth.

Genesis 1.2

וְהָאָרֶץ הָיְתָה תֹהוּ וָבֹהוּ וְחשֶׁךְ עַל פְּנֵי תְהוֹם וְרוּחַ
אֱלֹהִים מְרַחֶפֶת עַל פְּנֵי הַמָּיִם

וְהָאָרֶץ (and the earth) is composed of the linking word וְ (and) and the feminine singular definite noun הָאָרֶץ (the earth). The verb הָיְתָה (it was) is a 3rd person feminine singular, Completed Action, Simple Mood from היה (to be); it is irregular (compare with the regular form (XXXה). תֹהוּ (desolation) is a masculine singular noun; וָבֹהוּ (and emptiness) is composed of the linking word וְ (and) and the masculine singular noun בֹהוּ (emptiness). וְחשֶׁךְ is composed of the linking word וְ (and) and the masculine singular noun חשֶׁךְ (darkness). Here the word 'was' is understood. עַל (upon) is a preposition. פְּנֵי (face) is a masculine plural noun – it is the first word of a Word Pair. תְהוֹם (deep) is a masculine singular noun and the second word of a Word Pair. It is definite but does not take הַ. The Word Pair פְּנֵי תְהוֹם thus means 'face of the deep'. וְרוּחַ (and the spirit of) is composed of the linking word וְ (and) and the feminine singular noun רוּחַ

which is the first word of a Word Pair. אֱלֹהִים (God) is the second word of the Word Pair וְרוּחַ אֱלֹהִים (and the spirit of God). מְרַחֶפֶת (hovering) is the 3rd person feminine, Continuing Action, Intensive Mood of רחף (hover). Again, עַל (upon) is a preposition. פְּנֵי (face of) is the first word of a Word Pair. הַמָּיִם (the waters) is a masculine plural definite noun and the second word of the Word Pair פְּנֵי הַמָּיִם (face of the waters).

> *And the earth was desolation and emptiness, and darkness was upon the face of the deep, and the Spirit of God hovering upon the face of the waters.*

Genesis 1.3

וַיֹּאמֶר אֱלֹהִים יְהִי אוֹר וַיְהִי אוֹר

וַיֹּאמֶר is composed of the linking word וַ (and) and the verb יֹּאמֶר, 3rd person masculine singular, Uncompleted Action, Simple Mood, from אמר. This is an irregular verb (compare the regular form XXXי).

Because the verb is preceded by וַ, the tense changes from Uncompleted to Completed: thus וַיֹּאמֶר means 'and he said'. אֱלֹהִים (God) is the name of God. The verb יְהִי is the 3rd person masculine singular, Uncompleted Action, Simple Mood, from היה. This is an irregular verb (compare the regular form XXXי). Here the verb has the force of a command – thus יְהִי means 'Let there be'. אוֹר (light) is a masculine singular noun. וַיְהִי is composed of the linking word וַ (and) and the same form יְהִי. Because וַ precedes the verb, the tense changes from Uncompleted to Completed Action. Thus וַיְהִי means 'and there was'. Again אוֹר means 'light'.

> *And God said, 'Let there be light'. And there was light.*

Genesis 1.4

וַיַּרְא אֱלֹהִים אֶת הָאוֹר כִּי טוֹב וַיַּבְדֵּל אֱלֹהִים בֵּין הָאוֹר וּבֵין הַחֹשֶׁךְ

וַיַּרְא (and he saw) is composed of the linking word וַ (and) and the verb יַרְא (he will see), 3rd person masculine singular, Uncompleted

Action, Simple Mood, from רָאָה (see). This is an irregular verb (compare the regular form XXX֣י). Because וַ precedes the main letters of the verb, the tense is reversed: thus וַיַּרְא means 'and he saw'. אֱלֹהִים (God) is the name of God. אֵת indicates that וַיַּרְא takes a definite direct object. הָאוֹר (the light) is a masculine singular definite noun. כִּי (that) is a relative pronoun. The phrase 'it was' is understood. טוֹב (good) is a masculine singular adjective referring back to הָאוֹר. וַיַּבְדֵּל is composed of the linking word וַ (and) and the verb יַבְדֵּל (and he divided), 3rd person singular, Uncompleted Action, Causative Mood, from בדל (divide). Again, אֱלֹהִים is the name of God. בֵּין (between) is a preposition. הָאוֹר (the light) again is a masculine singular definite noun. וּבֵין is composed of the linking word וּ (and) and the preposition בֵּין (between). הַחֹשֶׁךְ (the darkness) is a masculine singular definite noun.

And God saw the light that it was good, and he divided between the light and the darkness.

Genesis 1.5

וַיִּקְרָא אֱלֹהִים לָאוֹר יוֹם וְלַחֹשֶׁךְ קָרָא לָיְלָה וַיְהִי עֶרֶב
וַיְהִי בֹקֶר יוֹם אֶחָד

וַיִּקְרָא (and he called) is composed of the linking word וַ (and) and the verb יִקְרָא (he will call), 3rd person masculine singular, Uncompleted Action, Simple Mood from קרא (call). This is an irregular verb (compare the regular form XXX֣י). Because וַ precedes the main letters of the verb, the tense is reversed; thus וַיִּקְרָא means 'and he called'. אֱלֹהִים (God) is the name of God. לָאוֹר is composed of the preposition ל (which is used in connection with the verb קרא but is not translated) and the masculine singular noun אוֹר (light). The Qames under the ל indicates that אוֹר is definite. יוֹם (day) is a masculine singular noun. וְלַחֹשֶׁךְ is composed of וְ (and), the preposition ל (used after קרא but not translated), and the masculine singular noun חֹשֶׁךְ (darkness). The Patah (X) under ל indicates that חֹשֶׁךְ is definitive. The verb קָרָא (he called) is 3rd person masculine singular, Completed Action, Simple Mood, from קרא (call). This is an irregular verb (compare the regular form XXX). לָיְלָה (night) is a masculine singular noun. וַיְהִי (and there was) is composed of

וֹ (and) and the verb יְהִי (it will be), 3rd person masculine singular, Uncompleted Action, Simple Mood from היה (to be). This is an irregular verb (compare XXיֹ). Because וֹ precedes the main letters of the verb, the tense is reversed: thus וַיְהִי means 'and it was'. עֶרֶב (evening) is a masculine singular noun. וַיְהִי (and it was) is repeated. בֹּקֶר (morning) is a masculine singular noun. יוֹם (day) is a masculine singular noun. אֶחָד (one) is a masculine singular adjective.

And God called the light day, and the darkness he called night. And it was evening, and was morning, one day.

CHAPTER TWENTY-SIX

Adam (Genesis 2.15–18)

Genesis 2.15

וַיִּקַּח יְהוָה אֱלֹהִים אֶת הָאָדָם וַיַּנִּחֵהוּ בְגַן עֵדֶן לְעָבְדָהּ
וּלְשָׁמְרָהּ

וַיִּקַּח is composed of the linking word וְ (and) and the verb יִקַּח (he will take), 3rd person masculine singular, Uncompleted Action, Simple Mood, from לקח (take). This is an irregular verb (compare the regular form xxx). Because וְ precedes the main letters of the verb, the tense is reversed. Thus וַיִּקַּח means 'and he took'. יְהוָה (Lord) and אֱלֹהִים (God) are the names of God. אֶת indicates that וַיִּקַּח takes a direct object. הָאָדָם (the man) is a masculine singular definite noun. וַיַּנִּחֵהוּ is composed of the linking word וְ (and), the verb יַנִּחֵהוּ (he will place him), 3rd masculine singular, Uncompleted Action, Causative Mood, from נוח (place), and the 3rd masculine singular object pronoun. This is an irregular verb (compare the regular form xxx). Because וְ precedes the main letters of the verb, the tense is reversed. Thus וַיַּנִּחֵהוּ means 'he placed him'. בְגַן is composed of the preposition בְ (in) and the feminine singular noun גַּן (garden). This is the first word of a Word Pair. עֵדֶן (Eden) is a masculine singular noun and the second word in the Word Pair בְגַן עֵדֶן (in the garden of Eden). לְעָבְדָהּ (to cultivate it) is an Infinitive, Simple Mood, from עבד (work or cultivate) and the feminine object pronoun. וּלְשָׁמְרָהּ is composed of the linking word וְ (and) and an Infinitive, Simple Mood, from שמר (watch) with the feminine singular object pronoun.

And the Lord God took the man and he placed him in the garden of Eden to cultivate it and to watch over it.

Genesis 2.16

וַיְצַו יְהֹוָה אֱלֹהִים עַל הָאָדָם לֵאמֹר מִכֹּל עֵץ הַגָּן אָכֹל
תֹּאכֵל

וַיְצַו is composed of the linking word וַ (and) and the verb יְצַו (he will command), 3rd person masculine singular, Uncompleted Action, Intensive Mood, from צוה (command). This is an irregular verb (compare XXXְיַ). Because וַ precedes the main letters of the verb, the tense is reversed. Thus וַיְצַו means 'he commanded'. יְהֹוָה (Lord) is the name of God. עַל is the preposition which follows צוה and is not translated. הָאָדָם (the man) is a masculine singular definite noun. לֵאמֹר (to say) is an Infinitive, Simple Mood, from אמר (say). It is an irregular verb (compare XXXְל). Here it means 'saying'. מִכֹּל is composed of the preposition מִ (from) and the masculine singular noun כֹּל (every) which is the first word of a Word String. עֵץ (tree) is a masculine singular noun and the second word of a Word String. הַגָּן (the garden) is a masculine singular definite noun and the third word of the Word String מִכֹּל עֵץ הַגָּן (from every tree of the garden). אָכֹל is the emphatic Infinitive of אכל (eat). The verb תֹּאכֵל (you will eat) is 2nd person, masculine singular, Uncompleted Action, Simple Mood, from אכל. This is an irregular verb (compare XXXְתִּ).

The Lord God commanded the man saying, 'From every tree of the garden you will indeed eat.'

Genesis 2.17

וּמֵעֵץ הַדַּעַת טוֹב וָרָע לֹא תֹאכַל מִמֶּנּוּ כִּי בְּיוֹם אֲכָלְךָ
מִמֶּנּוּ מוֹת תָּמוּת

וּמֵעֵץ (but from the tree of) is composed of the linking word וּ (but), the preposition מֵ (from) and the masculine singular noun עֵץ (tree) – this is the first word of a Word String. הַדַּעַת (the knowledge of) is a feminine singular definite noun – it is the second word of a Word String. טוֹב (good) is a masculine singular noun – it is the third word of a Word String. וָרָע (and evil) is a masculine singular noun – it is the fourth word of a Word String. וּמֵעֵץ הַדַּעַת טוֹב וָרָע thus means 'but from the tree of the knowledge of good and evil'. לֹא (not) is an adverb. The verb תֹּאכַל (you will eat) is 2nd person masculine, Uncompleted Action, Simple Mood, from אכל (eat). מִמֶּנּוּ (from it) is composed of the preposition מ (from) and the 3rd person masculine singular object pronoun. כִּי (because) is a conjunction. בְּיוֹם (on the day of) is composed of the preposition בּ and the masculine singular noun יוֹם (day) – this is the first word of a Word Pair. אֲכָלְךָ (your eating) is composed of an Infinitive, Simple Mood from אכל (eat), with a 2nd person masculine singular possessive – it is the second word of the Word Pair בְּיוֹם אֲכָלְךָ (on the day of your eating). מִמֶּנּוּ again means 'from it'. מוֹת is an emphatic Infinitive, Simple Mood, from מות (die). It is an irregular verb (compare XXX). The verb תָּמוּת (you will die) is 2nd person, masculine singular, Uncompleted Action, Simple Mood, from מות (die). It is an irregular verb (compare XXXתִּ).

But from the tree of the knowledge of good and evil you will not eat from it, because on the day of your eating from it you will indeed die.

Genesis 2.18

וַיֹּאמֶר יְהוָֹה אֱלֹהִים לֹא טוֹב הֱיוֹת הָאָדָם לְבַדּוֹ אֶעֱשֶׂה לוֹ עֵזֶר כְּנֶגְדּוֹ

וַיֹּאמֶר is composed of the linking word וַ (and) and the verb יֹּאמֶר (he will say), 3rd person masculine singular, Uncompleted Action, Simple Mood, from אמר. This is an irregular verb (compare XXXיְ). יְהוָֹה (Lord) and אֱלֹהִים (God) are the names of God. לֹא (not) is an adverb. טוֹב (good) is a masculine singular adjective. The verb 'is' is understood. הֱיוֹת (being) is an Infinitive, Simple Mood, from היה – it is the first word of a Word Pair. This is an irregular verb (compare XXX). הָאָדָם (the man) is a masculine singular definite noun – it is the second word of the Word Pair הֱיוֹת הָאָדָם (being of the man). Here the meaning of הֱיוֹת הָאָדָם is 'for the man to be'. לְבַדּוֹ is composed of the preposition לְ (to), the masculine singular noun בַד (separation), and a 3rd person singular possessive וֹ (his). לְבַדּוֹ means 'alone'. The verb אֶעֱשֶׂה (I shall make) is 1st person singular, Uncompleted Action, Simple Mood from עשה (make). This is an irregular verb (compare XXXאֶ). לוֹ is composed of the preposition לְ (for) and the 3rd person masculine singular object pronoun.

עֵזֶר (help) is a masculine singular noun. כְּנֶגְדּוֹ is composed of the preposition כְּ (as), the preposition נֶגֶד (opposite) and the 3rd person masculine singular object pronoun. כְּנֶגְדּוֹ thus means 'opposite him'. The expression עֵזֶר כְּנֶגְדּוֹ means 'a helpmeet for him'.

> *The Lord God said, 'It is not good for the man to be alone. I will make a helpmeet for him.'*

CHAPTER TWENTY-SEVEN

Eve (Genesis 3.1–4)

Genesis 3.1

וְהַנָּחָשׁ הָיָה עָרוּם מִכֹּל חַיַּת הַשָּׂדֶה אֲשֶׁר עָשָׂה יְהוָה
אֱלֹהִים וַיֹּאמֶר אֶל הָאִשָּׁה אַף כִּי אָמַר אֱלֹהִים לֹא
תֹאכְלוּ מִכֹּל עֵץ הַגָּן

וְהַנָּחָשׁ is composed of the linking word וְ (and) and the masculine singular noun נָחָשׁ (serpent). The verb הָיָה (he was) is 3rd person masculine singular, Completed Action, Simple Mood from היה (to be). This is an irregular verb (compare XXX). עָרוּם (subtle) is a masculine singular adjective. מִכֹּל is composed of the preposition מ (from) and the masculine singular noun כֹּל. This is used to make a comparison and it is the first word of a Word String. חַיַּת (living thing) is a feminine singular noun – it is the second word of a Word String. הַשָּׂדֶה (the field) is a feminine singular definite noun. מִכֹּל חַיַּת הַשָּׂדֶה thus means 'more than every living thing of the field'. אֲשֶׁר (which) is a relative pronoun. The verb עָשָׂה (he made) is 3rd person masculine singular, Completed Action, Simple Mood from עשה (make). יְהוָה (Lord) and אֱלֹהִים (God) are the names of God. וַיֹּאמֶר is composed of the linking word וַ (and) and the verb יֹּאמֶר (he will say), 3rd person masculine singular, Uncompleted Action, Simple Mood from אמר (say). This is an irregular verb (compare XXXי). Because וַ precedes the main letters of the verb, the tense is reversed. Thus וַיֹּאמֶר means 'and he said'. אֶל is a preposition. הָאִשָּׁה (the woman) is a feminine singular definite noun. אַף (also) and כִּי (because) are conjunctions – together they mean 'indeed is it that?' The verb אָמַר (he said) is 3rd person masculine singular, Completed Action, Simple Mood from אמר (say). אֱלֹהִים (God) is the name of God. לֹא (not) is an adverb. The verb תֹאכְלוּ (you will eat) is 2nd person masculine plural, Uncompleted Action, Simple Mood, from אכל (eat). This is an irregular verb (compare תֹּXXXוּ). מִכֹּל is composed of the preposition מ and the masculine singular noun כֹּל (every) – this is the first word of a Word String. עֵץ (tree) is a masculine singular noun – it is the second word of a Word String. הַגָּן (the garden) is a masculine singular definite noun – it is the third word of the Word String מִכֹּל עֵץ הַגָּן (from every tree of the garden).

And the serpent was more subtle than every living thing of the field which the Lord God had made. And he said to the woman, 'Indeed is it that God said, "You will not eat from every tree of the garden"?'

Genesis 3.2

וַתֹּאמֶר הָאִשָּׁה אֶל הַנָּחָשׁ מִפְּרִי עֵץ הַגָּן נֹאכֵל

וַתֹּאמֶר is composed of the linking word וַ (and) and the verb תֹּאמֶר, 3rd person feminine singular, Uncompleted Action, Simple Mood from אמר (say). This is an irregular verb (compare תֹּאXXX). Because וַ precedes the main letters of the verb, the tense is reversed. Thus וַתֹּאמֶר means 'and she said'. הָאִשָּׁה (the woman) is a feminine singular definite noun. אֶל (to) is a preposition. הַנָּחָשׁ (the serpent) is a masculine singular definite noun. מִפְּרִי is composed of the preposition מִ (from) and the masculine singular noun פְּרִי (fruit) – this is the first word of a Word String. עֵץ (tree) is a masculine singular noun – it is the second word of a Word String. הַגָּן (the garden) is a masculine singular definite noun – it is the third word of the Word String מִפְּרִי עֵץ הַגָּן (from the fruit of the tree of the garden). The verb נֹאכֵל (we may eat) is 1st person plural, Uncompleted Action, Simple Mood from אכל (eat). This is an irregular verb (compare נֹXXX).

And the woman said to the serpent, 'From the fruit of the tree of the garden, we may eat.'

Genesis 3.3

וּמִפְּרִי הָעֵץ אֲשֶׁר בְּתוֹךְ הַגָּן אָמַר אֱלֹהִים לֹא תֹאכְלוּ
מִמֶּנּוּ וְלֹא תִגְּעוּ בּוֹ פֶּן תְּמֻתוּן

וּמִפְּרִי is composed of the linking word וּ (but), the preposition מ (from) and the masculine singular noun פְּרִי (fruit) – this is the first word of a Word Pair. הָעֵץ (the tree) is a masculine singular definite noun – it is the second word of the Word Pair וּמִפְּרִי הָעֵץ (but from

94

the fruit of the tree). אֲשֶׁר (which) is a relative pronoun. בְּתוֹךְ is composed of the preposition בּ (in), the masculine noun תוֹךְ (midst) – this is the first word of a Word Pair. הַגָּן (the garden) is a masculine singular noun – it is the second word of the Word Pair בְּתוֹךְ הַגָּן (in the midst of the garden). The verb אָמַר is 3rd person masculine singular, Completed Action, Simple Mood from אמר (say). אֱלֹהִים (God) is the name of God. לֹא (not) is an adverb. The verb תֹאכְלוּ (you may eat) is 2nd person plural, Uncompleted Action, Simple Mood from אכל. מִמֶּנּוּ is composed of the preposition מ (from) and the masculine singular object pronoun. מִמֶּנּוּ thus means 'from it'. וְלֹא is composed of the linking word וּ (and) and the adverb לֹא (not). The verb תִגְּעוּ (you may touch) is 2nd person plural, Uncompleted Action, Simple Mood from נגע (touch). This is an irregular verb (compare תִּXXX). בּוֹ is composed of the preposition בּ, which is used with the verb but is not translated, and the 3rd person masculine singular object pronoun וֹ (it). פֶּן (lest) is a conjunction. The verb תְּמֻתוּן (you will die) is 2nd person plural, Uncompleted Action, Simple Mood from מות. This is an irregular verb (compare תִּXXX).

But from the fruit of the tree which is in the midst of the garden, God said, 'You may not eat from it and you may not touch it lest you will die.'

Genesis 3.4

וַיֹּאמֶר הַנָּחָשׁ אֶל הָאִשָּׁה לֹא מוֹת תְּמֻתוּן

וַיֹּאמֶר is composed of the linking word וּ (and) and the verb יֹּאמֶר (he will say), 3rd person masculine singular, Uncompleted Action, Simple Mood, from אמר (say). This is an irregular verb (compare יִXXX). Because וּ precedes the main letters of the verb, the tense is reversed. Thus וַיֹּאמֶר means 'and he said'. הַנָּחָשׁ (the serpent) is a masculine singular definite noun. אֶל (to) is a preposition. הָאִשָּׁה (the woman) is a feminine singular definite noun. לֹא (not) is an adverb. מוֹת is the emphatic Infinitive, Simple Mood, from מות. This is an irregular verb (compare XXX). The verb תְּמֻתוּן is 2nd person plural, Uncompleted Action, Simple Mood from מות (die).

And the serpent said to the woman, 'You will indeed not die.'

CHAPTER TWENTY-EIGHT

Noah (Genesis 7.1–3)

Genesis 7.1

וַיֹּאמֶר יְהֹוָה לְנֹחַ בֹּא אַתָּה וְכָל בֵּיתְךָ אֶל הַתֵּבָה כִּי
אֹתְךָ רָאִיתִי צַדִּיק לְפָנַי בַּדּוֹר הַזֶּה

וַיֹּאמֶר is composed of the linking word וַ (and) and the verb יֹּאמֶר, 3rd person masculine singular, Uncompleted Action, Simple Mood, from אמר (say). This is an irregular verb (compare the regular form xxxי). Because it is preceded by וַ, the tense is reversed. Thus וַיֹּאמֶר means 'and he said.' יְהֹוָה (Lord) is the name of God. לְנֹחַ is composed of the preposition ל (to) and the noun נֹחַ (Noah). The verb בֹּא (come) is a masculine singular Command, Simple Mood, from בוא (come). This is an irregular verb (compare the regular form xxx). אַתָּה (you) is a 2nd person masculine singular pronoun. וְכָל (and all of) is composed of the linking word וְ (and) and the masculine singular noun כָל (all) – it is the first word of a Word Pair. בֵּיתְךָ (your house) is composed of the masculine noun בֵּית (house) with a 2nd person masculine singular possessive ךָ (your). It is the second word of the Word Pair וְכָל בֵּיתְךָ (and all of your house). אֶל (to) is a preposition. הַתֵּבָה (the Ark) is a feminine singular definite noun. כִּי (because) is a conjunction. אֹתְךָ (you) is a masculine singular object pronoun. The verb רָאִיתִי is 1st person singular, Completed Action, Simple Mood, from ראה (see). It is an irregular verb (compare the regular form xxxתִּי). The verb 'are' is understood. צַדִּיק (righteous) is a masculine singular adjective. לְפָנַי is composed of the preposition ל (to) and the masculine plural noun פָנַי (face) with the 1st person singular possessive Xי (my). לְפָנַי means 'before me'. בַּדּוֹר is composed of the preposition ב (in) and the masculine singular noun דּוֹר (generation). The Patah under the ב indicates that the noun is definite. הַזֶּה (this) is a masculine singular pointing adjective. בַּדּוֹר הַזֶּה thus means 'in this generation'.

And the Lord said to Noah, 'Come, you and all your house to the

Ark because I have seen you are righteous before me in this generation.'

Genesis 7.2

מִכֹּל הַבְּהֵמָה הַטְּהוֹרָה תִּקַּח לְךָ שִׁבְעָה שִׁבְעָה אִישׁ וְאִשְׁתּוֹ וּמִן הַבְּהֵמָה אֲשֶׁר לֹא טְהֹרָה הִוא שְׁנַיִם אִישׁ וְאִשְׁתּוֹ

מִכֹּל is composed of the preposition מ (from) and the masculine singular noun כֹּל (all) – this is the first word of a Word Pair. הַבְּהֵמָה (the cattle) is a feminine singular definite noun – it is the second word of the Word Pair מִכֹּל הַבְּהֵמָה (from all the cattle). הַטְּהוֹרָה (clean) is a feminine singular adjective. The verb תִּקַּח (you will take) is 2nd person masculine singular, Uncompleted Action, Simple Mood from לקח (take). This is an irregular verb (compare the regular form תִּ‌XXX). לְךָ is composed of the preposition ל (to) and the 2nd person masculine singular object pronoun ךָ (you). Here לְךָ is not translated. שִׁבְעָה (seven) is a masculine singular noun. The expression שִׁבְעָה שִׁבְעָה means 'seven pairs'. אִישׁ (man) is a masculine singular noun. וְאִשְׁתּוֹ is composed of the linking word וְ (and) and the feminine singular noun אִשְׁתּוֹ (his wife) with a 3rd person masculine singular possessive. The expression אִישׁ וְאִשְׁתּוֹ means 'a male and his mate'. וּמִן is composed of the linking word וּ (and) and the preposition מִן (from). הַבְּהֵמָה (the cattle) is a feminine singular noun. אֲשֶׁר (which) is a relative pronoun. לֹא (not) is an adverb. Here 'is' is understood. טְהֹרָה (clean) is a feminine singular adjective. הִוא (it) is a 3rd person feminine singular pronoun – the normal spelling is הִיא. שְׁנַיִם (two) is a feminine plural noun. Here שְׁנַיִם means 'a pair'. אִישׁ וְאִשְׁתּוֹ again means 'a male and his mate'.

From all of the clean cattle you will take seven pairs, a male and his mate, and from the cattle which is not clean, a pair, a male and his mate.

Genesis 7.3

גַּם מֵעוֹף הַשָּׁמַיִם שִׁבְעָה שִׁבְעָה זָכָר וּנְקֵבָה לְחַיּוֹת זֶרַע
עַל פְּנֵי כָל הָאָרֶץ

גַּם (also) is an adverb. מֵעוֹף is composed of the preposition מ (from) and the masculine singular noun עוֹף (fowl) – this is the first word of a Word Pair. הַשָּׁמַיִם (heavens) is a masculine plural definite noun – it is the second word of the Word Pair מֵעוֹף הַשָּׁמַיִם (from the fowl of the heavens). שִׁבְעָה שִׁבְעָה again means 'seven pairs'. זָכָר (male) is a masculine singular noun. וּנְקֵבָה is composed of the linking word וּ (and) and a feminine singular noun נְקֵבָה (female). לְחַיּוֹת (to keep alive) is an Infinitive, Intensive Mood, from חיה (keep alive). This is an irregular verb (compare the regular form לְXXX). זֶרַע (seed) is a masculine singular noun. עַל (upon) is a preposition. פְּנֵי (face of) is a masculine plural noun – it is the first word of a Word String. כָל (all) is the second word of a Word String. הָאָרֶץ (the earth) is a feminine singular definite noun – it is the third word of the Word String פְּנֵי כָל הָאָרֶץ (the face of all of the earth).

Also from the fowl of the heavens, seven pairs, male and female, to keep alive seed upon the face of all of the earth.

CHAPTER TWENTY-NINE

Abraham and Isaac
(Genesis 22.1–3)

Genesis 22.1

וַיְהִי אַחַר הַדְּבָרִים הָאֵלֶּה וְהָאֱלֹהִים נִסָּה אֶת אַבְרָהָם
וַיֹּאמֶר אֵלָיו אַבְרָהָם וַיֹּאמֶר הִנֵּנִי

וַיְהִי is composed of the linking word וַ (and) and the verb יְהִי (it will be) 3rd person masculine singular, Uncompleted Action, Simple Mood, from היה (to be). This is an irregular verb (compare the regular form XXXיִ). Because וַ precedes the main consonants of the verb, the tense is reversed. Thus וַיְהִי means 'and it was'. אַחַר (after) is a preposition. הַדְּבָרִים (the things) is a masculine plural definite noun. הָאֵלֶּה (these) is a masculine plural pointing adjective. וְהָאֱלֹהִים is composed of the linking word וַ (here it means 'that'), and the masculine singular noun הָאֱלֹהִים (God). The verb נִסָּה (he tested) is 3rd person masculine singular, Completed Action, Intensive Mood from נסה (test). It is an irregular verb (compare the regular form XXX). אֶת indicates that נִסָּה takes a direct object. אַבְרָהָם (Abraham) is a masculine noun. וַיֹּאמֶר is composed of the linking word וַ (and) and the verb יֹאמֶר (he will say), 3rd person masculine singular, Uncompleted Action, Simple Mood, from אמר (say). It is an irregular verb (compare the regular form XXXיִ). אֵלָיו is composed of the preposition אֶל (to) and the 3rd person masculine singular object pronoun. אֵלָיו thus means 'to him'. אַבְרָהָם again means 'Abraham'. וַיֹּאמֶר again means 'and he said'. הִנֵּנִי is composed of the word הִנֵּה (behold!) and the 1st person singular object pronoun. הִנֵּנִי means 'behold me!' or 'here am I'.

And it was after these things that God tested Abraham, and he said to him, 'Abraham'. And he said, 'Here am I.'

Genesis 22.2

וַיֹּאמֶר קַח נָא אֶת בִּנְךָ אֶת יְחִידְךָ אֲשֶׁר אָהַבְתָּ אֶת
יִצְחָק וְלֶךְ לְךָ אֶל אֶרֶץ הַמֹּרִיָּה וְהַעֲלֵהוּ שָׁם לְעֹלָה עַל
אַחַד הֶהָרִים אֲשֶׁר אֹמַר אֵלֶיךָ

וַיֹּאמֶר is composed of the linking word וַ (and) and the verb יֹּאמֶר (he will say), 3rd person masculine singular, Uncompleted Action, Simple Mood, from אמר (say). Because וַ precedes the verb, the tense is reversed. Thus וַיֹּאמֶר means 'and he said'. The verb קַח is a 2nd person masculine singular, Command, Simple Mood from לקח (take). This is an irregular verb (compare the regular form XXX). The word נָא means 'I pray'. אֶת indicates that קַח takes a definite object. בִּנְךָ is composed of the masculine singular noun בֵּן and the 2nd person singular possessive ךָ (your). בִּנְךָ thus means 'your son'. אֶת again indicates that קַח takes a direct object. יְחִידְךָ is composed of the word יָהִיד (only one) and the 2nd person masculine singular possessive ךָ (your). יְחִידְךָ thus means 'your only one'. אֲשֶׁר (whom) is a relative pronoun. The verb אָהַבְתָּ (you loved) is 2nd person masculine singular, Completed Action, Simple Mood from אהב (love). אֶת again indicates a direct object of קַח. יִצְחָק means Isaac. וְלֶךְ is composed of the linking word וַ (and) and the verb לֶךְ (go!), 2nd person singular, Command, Simple Mood from הלך (go). This is an irregular verb (compare the regular form XXX). לְךָ is composed of the preposition לְ (to) and the 2nd person singular object pronoun – it is not translated. אֶל (to) is a preposition. אֶרֶץ (land of) is a feminine singular noun – it is the first word of a Word Pair. הַמֹּרִיָּה means Moriah – the Word Pair אֶרֶץ הַמֹּרִיָּה means 'the land of Moriah'. וְהַעֲלֵהוּ is composed of the linking word וַ (and) and the verb הַעֲלֵהוּ (sacrifice him), 2nd person masculine singular, Command, Causative Mood from עלה (sacrifice) with a 3rd person masculine singular object pronoun. This is an irregular verb (compare the regular form XXX(הַ)). שָׁם (there) is an adverb. לְעֹלָה is composed of the preposition לְ (for) and the feminine singular noun עֹלָה (offering). עַל (upon) is a preposition. אַחַד (one of) is the first word of a Word Pair. הֶהָרִים (the mountains) is a masculine plural noun – it is the second word of the Word Pair אַחַד הֶהָרִים (one of the mountains). אֲשֶׁר (which) is a relative pronoun. The verb אֹמַר is 1st person singular, Uncompleted

100

Action, Simple Mood from אמר (say). It is an irregular verb (compare the regular form XXXאֶ). אֵלֶיךָ is composed of the preposition אֶל (to) and the 2nd person masculine singular pronoun ךָ (you). אֵלֶיךָ thus means 'to you'.

> *And he said, 'Take I pray your son, your only one whom you loved, Isaac, and go to the land of Moriah, and sacrifice him there for an offering on one of the mountains which I will say to you.'*

Genesis 22.3

וַיַּשְׁכֵּם אַבְרָהָם בַּבֹּקֶר וַיַּחֲבֹשׁ אֶת חֲמֹרוֹ וַיִּקַּח אֶת שְׁנֵי
נְעָרָיו אִתּוֹ וְאֵת יִצְחָק בְּנוֹ וַיְבַקַּע עֲצֵי עֹלָה וַיָּקָם וַיֵּלֶךְ
אֶל הַמָּקוֹם אֲשֶׁר אָמַר לוֹ הָאֱלֹהִים

וַיַּשְׁכֵּם is composed of the linking word וֹ (and) and the verb יַשְׁכֵּם, 3rd person masculine singular, Uncompleted Action, Causative Mood from שׁכם (rise early). Because it is preceded by וֹ, the tense is reversed. Thus וַיַּשְׁכֵּם means 'and he arose'. אַבְרָהָם is the name 'Abraham'. בַּבֹּקֶר is composed of the preposition בַּ (in) and the definite, masculine singular noun בֹּקֶר (morning). וַיַּחֲבֹשׁ is composed of the linking word וֹ (and) and the verb יַחֲבֹשׁ, 3rd person masculine singular, Uncompleted Action, Simple Mood, from חבשׁ (saddle). אֶת indicates a direct object. חֲמֹרוֹ (his ass) is composed of a masculine singular noun and a 3rd person masculine singular possessive. וַיִּקַּח is composed of the linking word וֹ (and) and the verb יִקַּח, 3rd person masculine singular, Uncompleted Action, Simple Mood from לקח (take). This is an irregular verb (compare the regular form XXXי). Because it is preceded by וֹ, the tense is reversed. Thus וַיִּקַּח means 'and he took'. אֶת is the sign of the direct object. שְׁנֵי (two of) is a masculine plural noun; it is the first word of a Word Pair. נְעָרָיו (his youths) is composed of a masculine plural noun with a 3rd person masculine singular possessive pronoun. אִתּוֹ (with him) is composed of a preposition and a 3rd person masculine singular object pronoun. וְאֵת is composed of the linking word וֹ (and) and the sign of the direct object. יִצְחָק is the name 'Isaac'. בְּנוֹ (his son) is composed of a masculine singular noun and a 3rd person possessive. וַיְבַקַּע is composed of the linking word וֹ (and) and the verb יְבַקַּע, 3rd person masculine singular, Uncompleted Action, Intensive Mood

from בקע (cut). This is an irregular verb (compare the regular form
XXX). Because it is preceded by וֹ, the tense is reversed. Thus וַיְבַקַּע
means 'and he cut'. עֲצֵי (wood of) is a masculine plural noun – it
is the first word of a Word Pair. עלָה (burnt offering) is a feminine
singular noun – it is the second word of the Word Pair עֲצֵי עלָה
(wood of a burnt offering). וַיָּקָם is composed of the linking word וֹ
(and) and the verb יָקֻם (he will rise) 3rd person masculine singular, Uncompleted Action, Simple Mood, from קום (rise). This is an
irregular verb (compare the regular form XXX). Because וֹ precedes
the verb, the tense is reversed. Thus וַיָּקָם means 'and he rose'. וַיֵּלֶךְ
is composed of the linking word וֹ (and) and the verb יֵלֵךְ (he will
go), 3rd person masculine singular, Uncompleted Action, Simple
Mood, from הלך. This is an irregular verb (compare XXX). Because
it is preceded by וֹ, the tense is reversed. Thus וַיֵּלֶךְ means 'he went'.
אֶל (to) is a preposition. הַמָּקוֹם (the place) is a masculine singular
definite noun. אֲשֶׁר (which) is a relative pronoun. The verb אָמַר (he
said) is 3rd person masculine singular, Completed Action, Simple
Mood, from אמר (say). לוֹ is composed of the preposition ל (to) and
the 3rd person masculine singular object pronoun וֹ (him). אֱלֹהִים
(God) is the name of God.

*And Abraham arose in the morning, and he saddled his ass, and he
took two of his youths with him and Isaac his son. And he cut wood
of a burnt offering, and he rose, and he went to the place which God
said to him.*

Jacob (Genesis 28.10–12)

Genesis 28.10

וַיֵּצֵא יַעֲקֹב מִבְּאֵר שָׁבַע וַיֵּלֶךְ הָרָנָה

וַיֵּצֵא is composed of the linking word וֹ (and) and יֵּצֵא, 3rd person masculine singular, Uncompleted Action, Simple Mood, from יצא (go out). This is an irregular verb (compare the regular form xxẍ). Because it is preceded by וֹ, the tense is reversed. Thus וַיֵּצֵא means 'he went out'. יַעֲקֹב is the name 'Jacob'. מִבְּאֵר שָׁבַע is composed of the preposition מ (from) and the name בְּאֵר שָׁבַע (Beersheba). וַיֵּלֶךְ is composed of the linking word וֹ (and) and יֵּלֶךְ (he will go), 3rd person masculine singular, Uncompleted Action, Simple Mood, from הלך (go). This is an irregular verb (compare the regular form xxẍ). Because it is preceded by וֹ, the tense is reversed. Thus וַיֵּלֶךְ means 'and he went'. הָרָנָה (towards Haran) is a masculine singular noun – הָ at the end indicates direction.

And Jacob went out from Beersheba, and he went towards Haran.

Genesis 28.11

וַיִּפְגַּע בַּמָּקוֹם וַיָּלֶן שָׁם כִּי בָא הַשֶּׁמֶשׁ וַיִּקַּח מֵאַבְנֵי הַמָּקוֹם וַיָּשֶׂם מְרַאֲשֹׁתָיו וַיִּשְׁכַּב בַּמָּקוֹם הַהוּא

וַיִּפְגַּע is composed of the linking word וֹ (and) and יִּפְגַּע, 3rd person masculine singular, Uncompleted Action, Simple Mood, from פגע (reach). This is an irregular verb (compare the regular form xxẍ). Because it is preceded by וֹ, the tense is reversed. Thus וַיִּפְגַּע means 'and he reached'. בַּמָּקוֹם is composed of the preposition בּ, which is not translated, and the masculine singular noun מָקוֹם (place). Because there is a Patah (x̱) under the בּ, the noun is definite. וַיָּלֶן is composed of the linking word וֹ (and) and יָּלֶן, 3rd person masculine singular, Uncompleted Action, Simple Mood, from לון (lodge). This is an irregular verb (compare the regular form xxẍ). Because it is preceded by וַ, the tense is reversed. Thus וַיָּלֶן means 'and he lodged'. שָׁם (there) is an adverb. כִּי (because) is a linking word. The verb בָּא (came) is 3rd person masculine singular, Completed Action, Simple Mood, from בוא (come). This is an irregular verb (compare the regular form XXX). הַשֶּׁמֶשׁ (the sun) is a masculine singular definite noun. וַיִּקַּח is composed of the linking word וַ (and) and יִקַּח, 3rd person masculine singular, Uncompleted Action, Simple Mood, from לקח (take). This is an irregular verb (compare XXXי). Because it is preceded by וַ, the tense is reversed. Thus וַיִּקַּח means 'and he took'. מֵאַבְנֵי is composed of the preposition מ (from) and the masculine plural noun אַבְנֵי (stones of) – this is the first word of a Word Pair. הַמָּקוֹם again means 'the place' – this is the second word of the Word Pair מֵאַבְנֵי הַמָּקוֹם (from the stones of the place). וַיָּשֶׂם is composed of the linking word וַ (and) and יָשֶׂם, 3rd person masculine singular, Uncompleted Action, Simple Mood, from שׂים (put). This is an irregular verb (compare the regular form XXXי). Because it is preceded by וַ, the tense is reversed. Thus וַיָּשֶׂם means 'and he put'. מְרַאֲשֹׁתָיו (his head-stones) is a feminine plural noun with a 3rd person masculine singular possessive ו (his). וַיִּשְׁכַּב is composed of וַ (and) and יִשְׁכַּב, 3rd person masculine singular, Uncompleted Action, Simple Mood, from שכב (lie down). Because it is preceded by וַ, the tense is reversed. Thus וַיִּשְׁכַּב means 'and he lay down'. בַּמָּקוֹם (in the place) is composed of the preposition ב (in) and the masculine singular noun מָקוֹם (place). The Patah (X) under the ב indicates that the noun is definite. הַהוּא is a masculine singular pointing adjective.

And he reached the place, and he lodged there because the sun went down, and he took from the stones of the place, and put them at his head, and he lay down in that place.

Genesis 28.12

וַיַּחֲלֹם וְהִנֵּה סֻלָּם מֻצָּב אַרְצָה וְרֹאשׁוֹ מַגִּיעַ הַשָּׁמָיְמָה
וְהִנֵּה מַלְאֲכֵי אֱלֹהִים עֹלִים וְיֹרְדִים בּוֹ

וַיַּחֲלֹם is composed of the linking word וַ (and) and יַחֲלוֹם, 3rd person masculine singular, Uncompleted Action, Simple Mood from חלם (dream). This is an irregular verb (compare the regular form XXXי).

Because it is preceded by וֹ, the tense is reversed. Thus וַיַּחֲלֹם means 'he dreamed'. וְהִנֵּה is composed of וֹ (and) and the interjection הִנֵּה (behold). סֻלָּם (ladder) is a masculine singular noun. The verb מֻצָּב (set up) is 3rd person masculine singular, Completed Action, Passive Causative Mood, from נצב (set up). אַרְצָה (on earth) is a feminine singular noun. הX at the end indicates direction. וְרֹאשׁוֹ is composed of the linking word וֹ (and) and a masculine singular noun רֹאשׁוֹ (his head) with a 3rd person masculine possessive וֹ. The verb מַגִּיעַ (reaching) is 3rd person masculine singular, Continous Action, Causative Mood, from נגע (reach). This is an irregular verb (compare the regular form מַXXXיה). הַשָּׁמָיְמָה (to heaven) is a masculine plural noun. הX at the end indicates direction. וְהִנֵּה again means 'and behold'. מַלְאַכֵי (messengers of) is a masculine plural noun – it is the first word of a Word Pair. אֱלֹהִים (God) is the name of God – it is the second word of the Word Pair מַלְאַכֵי אֱלֹהִים (messengers of God). The verb עֹלִים (going up) is 3rd person plural, Continuous Action, Simple Mood, from עלה (go up). וְיֹרְדִים is composed of the linking word וֹ (and) and יֹרְדִים (descending), 3rd person plural, Continuous Action, Simple Mood, from ירד (descend). בּוֹ is composed of the preposition בּ and the 3rd person masculine singular object pronoun וֹ.

And he dreamed, and behold a ladder was set up on earth, with its head reaching to heaven, and behold the messengers of God ascending and descending on it.

CHAPTER THIRTY-ONE

Joseph (Genesis 45.4–7)

Genesis 45.4

וַיֹּאמֶר יוֹסֵף אֶל אֶחָיו גְּשׁוּ נָא אֵלַי וַיִּגָּשׁוּ וַיֹּאמֶר אֲנִי
יוֹסֵף אֲחִיכֶם אֲשֶׁר מְכַרְתֶּם אֹתִי מִצְרָיְמָה

וַיֹּאמֶר is composed of the linking word וַ (and) and the verb יֹּאמֶר, 3rd person masculine singular, Uncompleted Action, Simple Mood, from אמר (say). This is an irregular verb (compare the regular form xxxיׁ). Because it is preceded by וַ, the tense is reversed. Thus וַיֹּאמֶר means 'and he said'. יוֹסֵף (Joseph) is a noun. אֶל (to) is a preposition. אֶחָיו (his brothers) is composed of a masculine plural noun and a 3rd person masculine singular possessive. The verb גְּשׁוּ (draw near!) is a 2nd person plural Command, Simple Mood, from נגש (draw near). This is an irregular verb (compare the regular form xxx). נָא (I pray) is an interjection. אֵלַי is composed of the preposition אֶל (to) and a 1st person singular object pronoun. וַיִּגָּשׁוּ is composed of the linking word וַ (and) and the verb יִּגָּשׁוּ, 3rd person masculine plural, Uncompleted Action, Simple Mood, from נגש (draw near). This is an irregular verb (compare the regular form xxxיׁ). Because it is preceded by וַ, the tense is reversed. Thus וַיִּגָּשׁוּ means 'and they drew near'. וַיֹּאמֶר again means 'and he said'. אֲנִי (I) is a 1st person singular pronoun. 'Am' is understood. יוֹסֵף again means 'Joseph'. אֲחִיכֶם (your brother) is composed of a masculine singular noun and a 2nd person masculine plural possessive. אֲשֶׁר (whom) is a relative pronoun. The verb מְכַרְתֶּם (you sold) is 2nd person masculine plural, Completed Action, Simple Mood from מכר (sell). אֹתִי (me) is a 1st person singular object pronoun. מִצְרָיְמָה (Egypt) is a noun – הָX at the end indicates direction.

And Joseph said to his brothers, 'Draw near, I pray you, to me.'
And they drew near. And he said, 'I am Joseph your brother whom
you sold to Egypt.'

Genesis 45.5

וְעַתָּה אַל תֵּעָצְבוּ וְאַל יִחַר בְּעֵינֵיכֶם כִּי מְכַרְתֶּם אֹתִי
הֵנָּה כִּי לְמִחְיָה שְׁלָחַנִי אֱלֹהִים לִפְנֵיכֶם

וְעַתָּה is composed of the linking word וְ (and) and the adverb עַתָּה (now). אַל (not) is an adverb. The verb תֵּעָצְבוּ (you will be grieved) is 2nd person masculine plural, Uncompleted Action, Passive Simple Mood, from עצב (be grieved). This is an irregular verb (compare the regular form תֵּ XXX). וְאַל is composed of the linking word וְ (and) and the adverb אַל (not). The verb יִחַר is 3rd person masculine singular, Uncompleted Action, Simple Mood, from חרה (burn with anger). בְּעֵינֵיכֶם (in your eyes) is composed of the preposition בְּ (in) and a masculine plural noun with a 2nd person masculine plural possessive. יִחַר בְּעֵינֵיכֶם means 'and you will not be angry with yourselves'. כִּי (because) is a linking word. Again the verb מְכַרְתֶּם means 'you sold', and אֹתִי means 'me'. הֵנָּה (hither) is an adverb. כִּי here means 'since'. לְמִחְיָה is composed of the preposition לְ (for) and the feminine singular noun מִחְיָה (preservation of life). The verb שְׁלָחַנִי (sent me) is 3rd person singular, Completed Action, Simple Mood, from שלח (send), and a 1st person singular object pronoun. אֱלֹהִים (God) is the name of God. לִפְנֵיכֶם (before you) is composed of the preposition לִפְנֵי (before) and a 2nd person masculine plural object pronoun.

'And now, you should not be grieved, and you should not be angry with yourselves because you sold me hither, since God sent me for a preservation of life before you.'

Genesis 45.6

כִּי זֶה שְׁנָתַיִם הָרָעָב בְּקֶרֶב הָאָרֶץ וְעוֹד חָמֵשׁ שָׁנִים
אֲשֶׁר אֵין חָרִישׁ וְקָצִיר

כִּי (because) is a linking word. זֶה is a masculine singular pronoun. שְׁנָתַיִם (two years) is a feminine plural noun. זֶה שְׁנָתַיִם means 'these two years'. הָרָעָב (the famine) is a masculine singular definite noun. 'Was' is understood. בְּקֶרֶב (in the midst of) is composed of the preposition בְּ (in) and the masculine singular noun קֶרֶב (midst) – it is the first word of a Word Pair. הָאָרֶץ (the land) is a feminine singular definite noun – it is the second word of the Word Pair בְּקֶרֶב הָאָרֶץ (in the midst of the land). וְעוֹד is composed of the linking word וְ (and) and the adverb עוֹד (yet). חָמֵשׁ (five) is a feminine singular noun – it is the first word of a Word Pair. שָׁנִים (years) is a feminine plural noun – it is the second word of the Word Pair חָמֵשׁ שָׁנִים (five years). אֲשֶׁר (which) is a relative pronoun. אֵין means 'there will not be'. חָרִישׁ (ploughing) is a masculine singular noun. וְקָצִיר is composed of the linking word וְ (and) and the masculine singular noun קָצִיר (harvesting).

Because these two years the famine was in the midst of the land, and yet five years in which there will not be ploughing and harvesting.

Genesis 45.7

וַיִּשְׁלָחֵנִי אֱלֹהִים לִפְנֵיכֶם לָשׂוּם לָכֶם שְׁאֵרִית בָּאָרֶץ
וּלְהַחֲיוֹת לָכֶם לִפְלֵיטָה גְדֹלָה

וַיִּשְׁלָחֵנִי is composed of the linking word וַ (and) and the verb יִּשְׁלָחֵנִי, 3rd person masculine singular, Uncompleted Action, Simple Mood, from שלח (send), with a 1st person masculine singular object pronoun. Because it is preceded by וַ, the tense is reversed. Thus וַיִּשְׁלָחֵנִי means 'and he sent me'. אֱלֹהִים (God) is the name of God. לִפְנֵיכֶם (before you) is composed of the preposition לִפְנֵי (before) and the 2nd person masculine plural object pronoun. The verb לָשׂוּם (to put) is an Infinitive, Simple Mood, from שִׂים (put). This is an irregular verb (compare the regular form לXXX). לָכֶם is composed of the preposition לְ (to) and the 2nd person masculine plural object pronoun; here לְ is not translated. שְׁאֵרִית (remnant) is a feminine singular noun. בָּאָרֶץ (in the land) is composed of the preposition בְּ (in) and the feminine singular noun אֶרֶץ (land); because there is a Qames (X̱) under the בּ, it is definite. וּלְהַחֲיוֹת (and to cause to live) is composed of the linking word וּ (and) and an Infinitive, Causative Mood, from חיה (cause to live). This is an irregular verb (compare the regular form לְהַXXXY). לָכֶם again means 'to you'; it is not translated. לִפְלֵיטָה is composed of the preposition לְ (for) and the feminine singular noun פְּלֵיטָה (deliverance). גְדֹלָה (great) is a feminine singular adjective.

'And God sent me before you to put you as a remnant in the land and to keep you alive for a great deliverance.'

CHAPTER THIRTY-TWO

Moses (Exodus 3.2–4)

Exodus 3.2

וַיֵּרָא מַלְאַךְ יְהֹוָה אֵלָיו בְּלַבַּת אֵשׁ מִתּוֹךְ הַסְּנֶה וַיַּרְא
וְהִנֵּה הַסְּנֶה בֹּעֵר בָּאֵשׁ וְהַסְּנֶה אֵינֶנּוּ אֻכָּל

וַיֵּרָא is composed of the linking word וַ (and) and the verb יֵּרָא, 3rd person masculine singular, Uncompleted Action, Passive Simple Mood, from ראה (see). This is an irregular verb (compare the regular form XXXיִ). Because it is preceded by וַ, the tense is reversed. Thus וַיֵּרָא means 'and he appeared'. מַלְאַךְ (angel) is a masculine singular noun – it is the first word of a Word Pair. יְהֹוָה (Lord) is the name of God – it is the second word of the Word Pair מַלְאַךְ יְהֹוָה (an angel of the Lord). אֵלָיו (to him) is composed of the preposition אֶל (to) and a 3rd person masculine singular object pronoun. בְּלַבַּת (in a flame) is composed of the preposition בְּ (in) and the feminine singular noun לַבַּת (flame) – it is the first word of a Word Pair. אֵשׁ is a feminine singular noun – it is the second word of the Word Pair בְּלַבַּת אֵשׁ (in a flame of fire). מִתּוֹךְ (from the midst) is composed of the preposition מ (from) and the masculine singular noun תּוֹךְ (midst) – it is the first word of a Word Pair. הַסְּנֶה (the bush) is a masculine singular definite noun – it is the second word of the Word Pair מִתּוֹךְ הַסְּנֶה (from the midst of a thorn-bush). וַיַּרְא is composed of the linking word וַ (and) and the verb יַּרְא, 3rd person masculine singular, Uncompleted Action, Simple Mood, from ראה (see). It is an irregular verb (compare the regular form XXXיִ). Because it is preceded by וַ, the tense is reversed. Thus וַיַּרְא means 'and he saw'. וְהִנֵּה (and behold) is composed of the linking word וְ (and) and the interjection הִנֵּה (behold). הַסְּנֶה again means 'the bush'. The verb בֹּעֵר (burning) is 3rd person masculine singular, Continuing Action, Simple Mood, from בער (burn). בָּאֵשׁ is composed of the preposition בְּ (with) and the feminine singular noun אֵשׁ (fire). Because a Qames (X) is under the בְּ, the noun is definite. Thus בָּאֵשׁ means 'with the fire'. וְהַסְּנֶה is composed of the linking word וְ (but) and הַסְּנֶה (the bush). אֵינֶנּוּ is composed of the negation אֵין (there is not) and a 3rd person masculine singular pronoun. Thus אֵינֶנּוּ means 'it was not'. The verb אֻכָּל (being consumed) is a 3rd person masculine singular, Completed Action, Passive Intensive Mood, from אכל (eat).

> *And an angel of the Lord appeared to him in a flame of fire from the midst of the thorn-bush. And he saw. And behold, the thorn-bush burning with the fire, but the thorn-bush was not consumed.*

Exodus 3.3

וַיֹּאמֶר מֹשֶׁה אָסֻרָה נָּא וְאֶרְאֶה אֶת הַמַּרְאֶה הַגָּדֹל הַזֶּה
מַדּוּעַ לֹא יִבְעַר הַסְּנֶה

וַיֹּאמֶר is composed of the linking word וַ (and), and the verb יֹּאמֶר, 3rd person masculine singular, Uncompleted Action, Simple Mood, from אמר (say). It is an irregular verb (compare the regular form XXX'). Because it is preceded by וַ, the tense is reversed. Thus וַיֹּאמֶר means 'and he said'. מֹשֶׁה means 'Moses'. The verb אָסֻרָה is 1st person singular, Uncompleted Action, Simple Mood, from סור (turn aside). It is an irregular verb (compare the regular form XXX(אֶ)). נָּא (I pray) is an interjection; here it is not translated. וְאֶרְאֶה is composed of the linking word וְ (and) and the verb אֶרְאֶה, 1st person singular, Uncompleted Action, Simple Mood, from ראה (see). אֶת indicates that וְאֶרְאֶה takes a direct object. הַמַּרְאֶה (the sight) is a masculine singular definite noun. הַגָּדֹל (great) is a masculine singular definite adjective. הַזֶּה (this) is a masculine singular pointing adjective. מַדּוּעַ (why) is an adverb. לֹא (not) is an adverb. The verb יִבְעַר is 3rd person singular, Uncompleted Action, Simple Mood, from בער (burn). הַסְּנֶה again means 'the bush'.

> *And Moses said, 'I will turn aside and I will see this great sight why the thorn-bush is not burning.'*

Exodus 3.4

וַיַּרְא יְהוָה כִּי סָר לִרְאוֹת וַיִּקְרָא אֵלָיו אֱלֹהִים מִתּוֹךְ
הַסְּנֶה וַיֹּאמֶר מֹשֶׁה מֹשֶׁה וַיֹּאמֶר הִנֵּנִי

וַיַּרְא again means 'he saw'. יְהוָה (Lord) is the name of God. כִּי (that) is a linking word. The verb סָר (he turned) is 3rd person masculine singular, Completed Action, Simple Mood, from סור (turn). It is an irregular verb (compare the regular form XX̣X̣). לִרְאוֹת (to see) is an Infinitive, Simple Mood, from ראה (see). It is an irregular verb (compare the regular form XX̣X̣לְ). וַיִּקְרָא is composed of the linking word וַ and the verb יִּקְרָא, 3rd person masculine singular, Uncompleted Action, Simple Mood, from קרא (call). It is an irregular verb (compare the regular form XX̣X̣יְ). Because it is preceded by וַ, the tense is reversed. Thus וַיִּקְרָא means 'and he called'. אֵלָיו is composed of the preposition אֶל (to) and a 3rd person masculine singular object pronoun. אֱלֹהִים (God) is the name of God. מִתּוֹךְ הַסְּנֶה again means 'from the midst of the thorn-bush'. וַיֹּאמֶר again means 'and he said'. מֹשֶׁה means 'Moses'. וַיֹּאמֶר again means 'and he said'. הִנֵּנִי (here am I) is composed of an interjection הִנֵּה (behold) and a 3rd person masculine singular object pronoun.

And the Lord saw that he turned aside to see, and God called to him from the midst of the thorn-bush, and he said, 'Moses, Moses', and he said, 'Here am I'.

CHAPTER THIRTY-THREE

The Name of God
(Exodus 3.13–15)

Exodus 3.13

וַיֹּאמֶר מֹשֶׁה אֶל הָאֱלֹהִים הִנֵּה אָנֹכִי בָא אֶל בְּנֵי יִשְׂרָאֵל
וְאָמַרְתִּי לָהֶם אֱלֹהֵי אֲבוֹתֵיכֶם שְׁלָחַנִי אֲלֵיכֶם וְאָמְרוּ לִי
מַה שְּׁמוֹ מָה אֹמַר אֲלֵהֶם

וַיֹּאמֶר is composed of the linking word וַ (and) and the verb יֹּאמֶר,
3rd person masculine singular, Uncompleted Action, Simple Mood
from אמר (say). This is an irregular verb (compare the regular form
יxxx). Because it is preceded by וַ (and), the tense is reversed. Thus
וַיֹּאמֶר means 'and he said'. מֹשֶׁה means 'Moses'. אֶל (to) is a preposition. הָאֱלֹהִים (God) is the name of God. הִנֵּה (behold) is an interjection. אָנֹכִי (I) is a 1st person singular pronoun. The verb בָא (come) is
3rd person masculine singular, Continuous Action, Simple Mood,
from בוא (come). אֶל again means 'to'. בְּנֵי (children of) is a masculine plural noun – it is the first word of a Word Pair. יִשְׂרָאֵל means
'Israel' – it is the second word of the Word Pair בְּנֵי יִשְׂרָאֵל (the
children of Israel). וְאָמַרְתִּי is composed of the linking word וְ (and)
and the verb אָמַרְתִּי, 1st person singular, Completed Action, Simple Mood, from אמר (say). Because it is preceded by וְ, the tense is
reversed. Thus וְאָמַרְתִּי means 'and I will say'. לָהֶם (to them) is composed of the preposition ל (to) and a 3rd person masculine plural
object pronoun. אֱלֹהֵי (God of) is the first word of a Word Pair.
אֲבוֹתֵיכֶם (your fathers) is a masculine plural noun with a 2nd person masculine plural possessive – it is the second word of the Word
Pair אֱלֹהֵי אֲבוֹתֵיכֶם (the God of your fathers). The verb שְׁלָחַנִי (sent
me) is 3rd person masculine singular, Completed Action, Simple
Mood, from שלח (send), and a 1st person singular object pronoun.
אֲלֵיכֶם (to you) is composed of the preposition אֶל (to) and a 2nd person masculine plural object pronoun. וְאָמְרוּ is composed of the linking word וְ (and) and the verb אָמְרוּ, 3rd person masculine plural,

Completed Action, Simple Mood, from אמר (say). Because it is preceded by וֹ, the tense is reversed. Thus וְאָמְרוּ means 'and they will say'. לִי (to me) is composed of the preposition לְ (to) and a 1st person singular object pronoun. מַה (what) is a question pronoun. שְׁמוֹ (his name) is a masculine singular noun with a 3rd person masculine singular possessive. מָה again means 'what'. The verb אֹמַר (I will say) is 1st person singular, Uncompleted Action, Simple Mood, from אמר (say). It is an irregular verb (compare the regular form אֶXXX). אֲלֵהֶם (to them) is composed of the preposition אֶל (to) and the 3rd person masculine plural object pronoun.

> *And Moses said to God, 'Behold I come to the children of Israel, and I will say to them, "The God of your fathers has sent me to you." They will say to me, "What is his name?" What will I say to them?'*

Exodus 3.14

וַיֹּאמֶר אֱלֹהִים אֶל משֶׁה אֶהְיֶה אֲשֶׁר אֶהְיֶה וַיֹּאמֶר כֹּה
תֹאמַר לִבְנֵי יִשְׂרָאֵל אֶהְיֶה שְׁלָחַנִי אֲלֵיכֶם

וַיֹּאמֶר again means 'and he said'. אֱלֹהִים (God) is the Name of God. אֶל (to) is a preposition. משֶׁה means 'Moses'. The verb אֶהְיֶה is 1st person singular, Uncompleted Action, Simple Mood, from היה (to be). It is an irregular verb (compare the regular form אֶXXX). אֲשֶׁר (what) is a relative pronoun. אֶהְיֶה again means 'I will be'. וַיֹּאמֶר again means 'and he said'. כֹּה (thus) is an adverb. The verb תֹאמַר (you will say) is 2nd person masculine singular, Uncompleted Action, Simple Mood, from אמר (say). It is an irregular verb (compare the regular form תֶּXXX). לִבְנֵי (to the children of) is composed of the preposition לְ (to) and a masculine plural noun – it is the first word of a Word Pair. יִשְׂרָאֵל means 'Israel' – it is the second word of the Word Pair לִבְנֵי יִשְׂרָאֵל, 'to the children of Israel'. אֶהְיֶה again means 'I will be'. שְׁלָחַנִי again means 'he sent me'. אֲלֵיכֶם again means 'to you'.

> *And God said to Moses, 'I will be what I will be.' And he said, 'Thus you will say to the children of Israel, I will be sent me to you.'*

Exodus 3.15

וַיֹּאמֶר עוֹד אֱלֹהִים אֶל מֹשֶׁה כֹּה תֹאמַר אֶל בְּנֵי יִשְׂרָאֵל
יְהֹוָה אֱלֹהֵי אֲבֹתֵיכֶם אֱלֹהֵי אַבְרָהָם אֱלֹהֵי יִצְחָק וֵאלֹהֵי
יַעֲקֹב שְׁלָחַנִי אֲלֵיכֶם זֶה שְׁמִי לְעֹלָם וְזֶה זִכְרִי לְדֹר דֹּר

וַיֹּאמֶר again means 'and he said'. עוֹד (again) is an adverb. אֱלֹהִים
(God) is the name of God. אֶל (to) is a preposition. מֹשֶׁה means
'Moses'. כֹּה (thus) is an adverb. תֹאמַר again means 'you will say'.
אֶל again means 'to'. בְּנֵי יִשְׂרָאֵל again means 'children of Israel'.
יְהֹוָה (Lord) is the name of God. אֱלֹהֵי (God of) is the first word of a
Word Pair. אֲבֹתֵיכֶם (your fathers) is a masculine plural noun with a
2nd person masculine plural possessive – it is the second word of the
Word Pair אֱלֹהֵי אֲבֹתֵיכֶם (God of your fathers). אֱלֹהֵי אַבְרָהָם means
'the God of Abraham'. אֱלֹהֵי יִצְחָק means 'the God of Isaac'.
וֵאלֹהֵי יַעֲקֹב means 'and the God of Jacob'. שְׁלָחַנִי again means 'he sent me'.
אֲלֵיכֶם again means 'to you'. זֶה (this) is a masculine singular pointing pronoun. שְׁמִי (my name) is a masculine singular noun with a
1st person singular possessive. לְעֹלָם (for eternity) is composed of
the preposition ל (for) and the masculine singular noun עֹלָם (eternity). וְזֶה means 'and this'. זִכְרִי (my memorial) is a masculine singular noun with a 1st person singular possessive. לְדֹר is composed of
the preposition ל (for) and the masculine singular noun דֹר (generation). דֹר again means 'generation'.

*And God said again to Moses, 'Thus you will say to the children of
Israel, "The Lord the God of your Fathers, the God of Abraham,
the God of Isaac and the God of Jacob sent me to you." This is my
name for eternity, and this is my memorial from generation to
generation.'*

CHAPTER THIRTY-FOUR

Mt Sinai (Exodus 19.18–20)

Exodus 19.18

וְהַר סִינַי עָשַׁן כֻּלּוֹ מִפְּנֵי אֲשֶׁר יָרַד עָלָיו יהוה בָּאֵשׁ
וַיַּעַל עֲשָׁנוֹ כְּעֶשֶׁן הַכִּבְשָׁן וַיֶּחֱרַד כָּל הָהָר מְאֹד

וְהַר is composed of the linking word וְ (and) and the masculine singular noun הַר (mountain) – it is the first word of a Word Pair. סִינַי means 'Sinai' – it is the second word of the Word Pair הַר סִינַי (mountain of Sinai). The verb עָשַׁן (smoked) is 3rd person masculine singular, Completed Action, Simple Mood, from עשן (smoke). כֻּלּוֹ (all of it) is the masculine singular noun כֹּל (all) with a 3rd person masculine singular possessive. מִפְּנֵי is composed of the preposition מ (from) and the masculine plural noun פְּנֵי (faces of) – it is the first word of a Word Pair. אֲשֶׁר (which) is a relative pronoun – it is the second word of the Word Pair מִפְּנֵי אֲשֶׁר which here means 'because'. The verb יָרַד (descended) is 3rd person masculine singular, Completed Action, Simple Mood, from ירד (descend). עָלָיו (upon it) is composed of the preposition עַל (upon) and a 3rd person masculine singular object pronoun. יהוה (Lord) is the name of God. בָּאֵשׁ (in fire) is composed of the preposition בּ (in) and the feminine singular noun אֵשׁ (fire). וַיַּעַל is composed of the linking word וַ (and) and the verb יַּעַל, 3rd person masculine singular, Uncompleted Action, Simple Mood, from עלה (go up). It is an irregular verb (compare the regular form XXX). Because it is preceded by וַ, the tense is reversed. וַיַּעַל thus means 'and it went up'. עֲשָׁנוֹ (its smoke) is a masculine singular noun with a 3rd person masculine singular possessive. כְּעֶשֶׁן (like the smoke of) is composed of the preposition כּ (like) and the masculine singular noun עֶשֶׁן (smoke) – it is the first word of a Word Pair. הַכִּבְשָׁן (the furnace) is a masculine singular definite noun – it is the second word of the Word Pair כְּעֶשֶׁן הַכִּבְשָׁן (like the smoke of the furnace). וַיֶּחֱרַד is composed of the linking word וַ (and) and the verb יֶּחֱרַד, 3rd person masculine singular, Uncompleted Action, Simple Mood from חרד (tremble). It is an irregular verb (compare the regular form XXX‪יַ‬). Because it is preceded by וַ, the tense is reversed. Thus וַיֶּחֱרַד means 'and it trembled'. כָּל (all of) again is a masculine singular noun – it is the first word of a Word Pair. הָהָר (the mountain) is a masculine singular definite noun – it is the second word of the Word Pair כָּל הָהָר (all of the mountain). מְאֹד (greatly) is an adverb.

> *And Mount Sinai smoked all of it because the Lord descended upon it in the fire, and its smoke went up like the smoke of the furnace, and all of the mountain trembled greatly.*

Exodus 19.19

וַיְהִי קוֹל הַשֹּׁפָר הוֹלֵךְ וְחָזֵק מְאֹד מֹשֶׁה יְדַבֵּר וְהָאֱלֹהִים יַעֲנֶנּוּ בְקוֹל

וַיְהִי is composed of the linking word וַ (and) and the verb יְהִי, 3rd person masculine singular, Uncompleted Action, Simple Mood, from היה (to be). It is an irregular verb (compare the regular form XXX‪יַ‬). Because it is preceded by וַ, the tense is reversed. Thus וַיְהִי means 'and it was'. קוֹל (sound) is a masculine singular noun – it is the first word of a Word Pair. הַשֹּׁפָר (the shofar) is a masculine singular definite noun – it is the second word of the Word Pair קוֹל הַשֹּׁפָר, 'sound of the shofar'. The verb הוֹלֵךְ (going) is 3rd person masculine singular, Continuous Action, Simple Mood, from הלך (go). וְחָזֵק is composed of the linking word וְ (and) and the verb חָזֵק (growing stronger), 3rd person masculine singular, Continuous Action, Simple Mood from חזק (grow strong). מְאֹד (very) is an adverb. מֹשֶׁה means 'Moses'. The verb יְדַבֵּר is 3rd person masculine singular, Uncompleted Action, Intensive Mood from דבר (speak). וְהָאֱלֹהִים is composed of the linking word וְ (and) and הָאֱלֹהִים (God). The verb יַעֲנֶנּוּ (he answered him) is 3rd person masculine singular, Uncompleted Action, Simple Mood, from ענה (answer), with a 3rd person masculine singular object pronoun. It is an irregular form (compare the regular form XXX‪יַ‬). בְקוֹל is composed of the preposition ב (in) and the masculine singular noun קוֹל (voice).

> *And it was that the sound of the shofar was going out and growing stronger. Moses was speaking and the Lord was answering him in a voice.*

Exodus 19.20

וַיֵּרֶד יְהוָה עַל הַר סִינַי אֶל רֹאשׁ הָהָר וַיִּקְרָא יְהוָה
לְמֹשֶׁה אֶל רֹאשׁ הָהָר וַיַּעַל מֹשֶׁה

וַיֵּרֶד is composed of the linking word וַ (and) and the verb יֵרֶד, 3rd person masculine singular, Uncompleted Action, Simple Mood from ירד (descend). It is an irregular verb (compare the regular form XXXי). Because it is preceded by וַ, the tense is reversed. Thus וַיֵּרֶד means 'and he descended'. יְהוָה (Lord) is the name of God. עַל (upon) is a preposition. הַר סִינַי means 'Mt Sinai'. אֶל (to) is a preposition. רֹאשׁ (top) is a masculine singular noun – it is the first word of a Word Pair. הָהָר is a masculine singular definite noun – it is the second word of the Word Pair רֹאשׁ הָהָר, 'top of the mountain'. וַיִּקְרָא is composed of the linking word וַ (and) and the verb יִקְרָא, 3rd person masculine singular, Uncompleted Action, Simple Mood, from קרא (call). It is an irregular verb (compare the regular form XXXי). Because it is preceded by וַ, the tense is reversed. Thus וַיִּקְרָא means 'and he called'. לְמֹשֶׁה is composed of the preposition ל (to) and מֹשֶׁה (Moses). אֶל again means 'to'. רֹאשׁ הָהָר again means 'the top of the mountain'. וַיַּעַל again means 'and he went up'. מֹשֶׁה again means 'Moses'.

And the Lord descended upon Mt Sinai to the top of the mountain. And the Lord called to Moses to the top of the mountain. And Moses went up.

Reading the Hebrew Scriptures

You should now have an idea how to read the Hebrew Scriptures. We have covered the basic elements of Hebrew and analysed a number of important passages from Genesis and Exodus – this should have given you sufficient practice.

Let me make some suggestions how to get started. First you will need to purchase a Hebrew Bible – make sure that the title of each book in the Bible is in English, and that the chapters and verses are given in Roman numerals. This will make it much easier to find your place. (Hebrew Bibles are sometimes printed exclusively in Hebrew with Hebrew numbers.) You will also need to have Davidson's Lexicon at hand (as well as a simpler dictionary). Finally, you should place before you an English translation of the Bible and this book, too, in case you need to look up some grammatical points.

The Five Books of Moses are generally easier than many other books of the Bible, so why not begin with Genesis? I would recommend you choose passages you know and like, and see if you can translate them. Then move on to Exodus, Leviticus, Numbers and Deuteronomy. Be sure to select those sections that interest you most. You could then look at some of your favourite passages from the prophetic books as well as other books of the Bible. If you find the Hebrew too difficult, try something else: the aim should be to start reading! In case you need some suggestions, here is a list of passages you might like to read.

The golden calf	Exodus 32.15–20
God's glory	Exodus 33.17–23
Divorce	Deuteronomy 24.1–4
Covenant	Deuteronomy 29.11–14
Joshua	Deuteronomy 31.6–9
Samson and Delilah	Judges 16.15–19
Ruth	Ruth 1.16–18
Kingship	1 Samuel 8.4–8
David and Goliath	1 Samuel 17.48–51

Vocabulary

אָב (m) father
אֶבְיוֹן (m) poor
אֶבֶן (f) stone
אַבְרָהָם Abraham
אֱדוֹם (m) Edom
אָדוֹן (m) lord
אָדָם (m) man
אֲדָמָה (f) land
אהב love
אֲהָהּ alas
אֹהֶל (m) tent
אוֹר (m) light
אֹזֶן (f) ear
אָח (m) brother
אֶחָד (m) one
אַחַר after
אַיֵּה where
אֵין there is not
אִישׁ (m) man
אכל eat
אָכְלָה (f) food
אֶל unto
אַל not
אֵלֶּה (m) (f) these
אֵלִיָּהוּ Elijah
אֱלִיעֶזֶר Eliezer
אֵם (f) mother
אמר say
אֲנַחְנוּ (m) (f) we
אֲנִי (m) (f) I
אָנֹכִי I
אַף also
אַרְבַּע (f) four

אֲרִי (m) lion
אֶרֶץ (f) earth
אֵשׁ (f) fire
אִשָּׁה (f) woman
אַתְּ (fs) you
אַתָּה (ms) you
אָתוֹן (f) she-ass
אַתֶּם (mpl) you
אַתֵּן (fpl) you

בְּ in
בְּאֵר שֶׁבַע Beersheba
בֶּגֶד (m) garment
בדל divide
בֹּהוּ (m) emptiness
בְּהֵמָה (f) cattle
בוא come
בחר choose
בֵּין between
בַּיִת (m) house
בְּלִי without
בֵּן son
בער burn
בקע cleave
בָּקָר (m) (f) herd
בֹּקֶר (m) morning
בקשׁ seek
ברא create
בְּרָכָה (f) blessing
בַּת (f) daughter

גְּבוּל (m) border
גִּבּוֹר (m) hero

Vocabulary

גָּדוֹל	big, great	זכר	remember
גדל	be great	זָכָר	male
גּוֹי	(m) people, nation	זָקֵן	old
גַּם	also	זֶרַע	(m) seed
גַּן	(m) garden		
		חַג	(m) festival
דָּבָר	(m) word, thing	חֹדֶשׁ	(m) month
דבר	speak	חוּץ	except
דָּוִד	David	חזק	be strong
דּוֹר	(m) generation	חִטָּה	(f) wheat
דָּם	(m) blood	חַי	living
דַּעַת	(f) knowledge	חיה	live
דֶּרֶךְ	(m) (f) way	חַיִּים	(m) life
		חָכָם	wise
הָאֵלֶּה	(m) (f) these	חָכְמָה	(f) wisdom
הַהוּא	(m) that	חֲלוֹם	(m) dream
הוּא	he	חלם	dream
הַהִיא	(f) that	חָמֵשׁ	five
הָהֵם	(m) those	חֵן	(m) favour
הָהֵן	(f) those	חרד	tremble
הוֹלֵךְ	(m) walker	חרה	burn
הַזֹּאת	(f) this	חָרִישׁ	(m) ploughing
הַזֶּה	(m) this	חֹשֶׁךְ	(m) darkness
הִיא	she		
היה	to be	טָהוֹר	pure
הלך	go	טוֹב	good
הלל	praise	טוּר	(m) row
הֵם	(m) they		
הֵן	(f) they	יַבָּשָׁה	(f) dry land
הֵנָּה	(f) they	יָד	(f) hand
הֵנָּה	hither	ידע	know
הִנֵּה	behold	יְהוּדָה	Judah
הַר	mountain	יוֹם	(m) day
הֲרֵי	lo!	יוֹסֵף	Joseph
הָרָן	Haran	יוֹשֵׁב	(m) resident
		יָחִיד	only one
זֶה	(m) this	יַיִן	(m) wine
זֹאת	(f) this	יַלְדָּה	girl
זָהָב	(m) gold	יָם	(m) sea

121

יַעֲקֹב	Jacob		מְאֹד	very
יָפֶה	beautiful		מִדְבָּר	(m) desert
יָצָא	go out		מַדּוּעַ	why
יִצְחָק	Isaac		מָה	what
יִרְאָה	(f) fear		מוֹאָב	Moab
ירד	descend		מוּל	opposite
יְרוּשָׁלַיִם	Jerusalem		מוֹעֵד	(m) appointed time
ירש	inherit		מוֹשָׁב	(m) seat, settlement
יֵשׁ	there is		מות	die
ישב	dwell		מָוֶת	(m) death
יִשְׂרָאֵל	Israel		מִזְבֵּחַ	(m) altar
			מִחְיָה	(f) preservation of life
כְּ	as, like		
כַּאֲשֶׁר	as		מַחֲנֶה	(m) camp
כבד	honour		מִי	who
כָּבוֹד	(m) glory		מַיִם	(m) water
כִּבְשָׁן	(m) furnace		מכר	sell
כֹּה	thus		מַלְאָךְ	(m) messenger
כֹּהֵן	(m) priest		מִלָּה	(f) word
כּוֹכָב	(m) star		מִלְחָמָה	(f) war
כִּי	because		מלך	rule
כֹּל	all		מַלְכָּה	(f) queen
כַּמָּה	how much		מִן	from
כְּמוֹ	like		מְנוֹרָה	(f) candelabra
כִּסֵּא	(m) seat		מִסְפָּר	(m) number
כֶּסֶף	(m) silver		מַעֲשֶׂה	(m) deed
כתב	write		מִצְוָה	(f) commandment
			מִצְרַיִם	Egypt
לְ	to		מָקוֹם	(m) place
לֹא	not		מַקֵּל	(m) staff
לֵב	(m) heart		מִקְנֶה	(m) cattle
לוּחַ	(m) tablet		מַרְאֶה	(m) sight
לון	lodge		משֶׁה	Moses
לַיְלָה	(m) night		מִשְׁפָּחָה	(f) family
לָמָּה	why		מִשְׁפָּט	(m) judgement
לְמַעַן	in order that		
למד	learn		נָא	I pray
לִפְנֵי	before		נָבִיא	(m) prophet
לקח	take		נֶגֶד	opposite

נגע	reach	עָם	(m) people
נגשׁ	draw near	עמד	stand
נדף	smite	ענה	answer
נוח	rest	עָפָר	(m) dust
נוֹרָא	awesome	עֵץ	(m) tree
נֹחַ	Noah	עֶצֶם	(m) essence
נָחָשׁ	(m) serpent	עֶרֶב	(m) evening
נכה	smite	עָרוּם	subtle
נסה	test	עשׂה	do
נָעֳמִי	Naomi	עֵשָׂו	Esau
נַעַר	(m) youth	עשׁן	smoke
נפל	fall	עָשָׁן	(m) smoke
נצב	set up	עֲשָׂרָה	(m) ten
נְקֵבָה	female	עַתָּה	now
נתן	give		
		פגע	reach
סוּכָּה	booth	פֹּה	here
סוּס	(m) horse	פְּלֵטָה	(f) deliverance
סוּסָה	(f) mare	פְּלִשְׁתִּי	Philistine
סור	turn aside	פֶּן	lest
סִינַי	Sinai	פָּנִים	(m) face
סֻלָּם	(m) ladder	פֶּסַח	(m) Passover
סְנֶה	(m) thorn-bush	פַּעַם	occurrence
סֵפֶר	(m) book	פְּרִי	(m) fruit
		פַּרְעֹה	Pharaoh
עֶבֶד	(m) slave		
עבד	work	צֹאן	(m) (f) sheep
עֲבוֹדָה	(f) work	צַדִּיק	(m) righteous
עַד	until	צְדָקָה	(f) righteousness
עֵדֶן	Eden	צוה	command
עוֹד	yet	צוּר	rock
עוֹלָם	(m) eternity		
עָוֹן	(m) sin	קבל	receive
עוֹף	(m) fowl	קבר	bury
עֵזֶר	(m) help	קֶבֶר	(m) grave
עַיִן	(f) eye	קדשׁ	sanctify
עִיר	(f) city	קוֹל	(m) voice
עֹלָה	(f) offering	קָצִיר	(m) harvesting
עלה	go up	קרא	call

קֶרֶב	(m) midst		שָׁלוֹם	peace
			שׁלח	send
ראה	see		שְׁלֹשָׁה	(m) three
רֹאשׁ	head		שֵׁם	(m) name
רִאשׁוֹן	first		שָׁם	there
רֵאשִׁית	(f) beginning		שְׁמוּאֵל	Samuel
רַב	great		שָׁמַיִם	(m) heaven
רֶגֶל	(f) foot		שְׁמֹנָה	(m) eight
רוּחַ	(f) spirit		שׁמע	hear
רחף	hover		שׁמר	keep
רחץ	wash		שֹׁמֵר	(m) watchman
רַע	(m) evil		שֶׁמֶשׁ	(m) sun
רָעָב	(m) famine		שָׁנָה	(f) year
			שְׁנַיִם	(m) two
שָׁאוּל	Saul		שִׁשָּׁה	(m) six
שְׁאֵרִית	(f) remnant			
שֶׁבַע	seven		תֵּבָה	(f) ark
שׁבר	break		תֹּהוּ	(m) desolation
שָׂדֶה	field		תְּהוֹם	(m) deep
שׁוֹפֵט	(m) judge		תּוֹר	turtle dove
שׁוֹפָר	(m) shofar		תּוֹרָה	(f) law
שַׁחַר	(m) dawn		תָּוֶךְ	(m) midst
שׂים	put		תַּחַת	under
שִׁיר	(m) song		תְּפִלָּה	(f) prayer
שׁכב	lie down		תִּשְׁעָה	(m) nine

Answers to Exercises

Chapter 2

Exercise 2

1. adon
2. bayn
3. goyeem
4. dor
5. hakol
6. va
7. zehra
8. choots
9. toor
10. yam
11. kohayn
12. lo
13. nora
14. sooka
15. afar
16. pehsach
17. tsoor
18. kehvehr
19. reeshon
20. shabat

Chapter 3

Exercise 1

1.	Closed Syllable Closed Vowel זֶן	Open Syllable Open Vowel אָ
2.	Closed Syllable Closed Vowel כַר	Open Syllable Open Vowel יִ
3.	Closed Syllable Closed Vowel רַשׁ	Open Syllable Open Vowel יָ
4.	Closed Syllable Closed Vowel תַב	Open Syllable Open Vowel כָ

Exercise 2

1.	Closed Syllable Closed Vowel בֶן	Open Syllable Closed Vowel אֶ

2.	Closed Syllable Closed Vowel גַּד	Open Syllable Closed Vowel בְּ
3.	Closed Syllable Closed Vowel יִן	Open Syllable Closed Vowel יִ
4.	Closed Syllable Closed Vowel סַח	Open Syllable Closed Vowel פֶּ
5.	Closed Syllable Closed Vowel חַר	Open Syllable Closed Vowel שַׁ

Exercise 3

1. [טוֹב] [הַ][דָּ][בָר]
2. [לֹא] [אִישׁ] [אֶל]
3. [אֶ][ל][הִים] [בַּ][שָּׁ][מַ][יִם]

Chapter 4

Exercise 1

1. avraham
2. meetsva
3. malk@cha
4. yalda
5. avd@cha
6. tol@dot
7. paro
8. meelchama
9. mosh@vot
10. malka
11. yeekb@roo
12. yeeshm@roo
13. meekneh
14. meedbar
15. arba
16. sh@martehm
17. b@lee
18. yeera
19. b@racha

Exercise 2

1. anachnoo
2. yaakov
3. kaashehr
4. moadeem
5. machanot
6. maaseh
7. naamee
8. avadeem
9. avoda

Chapter 5

Exercise 1

1. ehvyon
2. adama
3. ahah
4. arba
5. b@hayma
6. bachar
7. bayeet
8. dam
9. zachar
10. kavod

11. meedbar
12. malka
13. meespar
14. meeshpat
15. nacha
16. nafal
17. sayfehr
18. paneem
19. tohoo
20. tachat

Exercise 2

1. ayyay
2. eeshsha
3. ayleeyyahoo
4. bama
5. geebbor
6. heennay
7. cheetta
8. yabbasha

9. kamma
10. keessay
11. lamma
12. meella
13. makkayl
14. meeshsham
15. atta

Chapter 6

Exercise 1

1. ehdom
2. ehchad
3. ehrehts
4. chag
5. har
6. am

7. avodah
8. l@maan
9. rachats
10. shachar
11. rooach
12. looach

Exercise 2

בְּרֵאשִׁית בָּרָא אֱלֹהִים אֵת הַשָּׁמַיִם וְאֵת הָאָרֶץ:
וְהָאָרֶץ הָיְתָה תֹהוּ וָבֹהוּ וְחֹשֶׁךְ עַל־פְּנֵי תְהוֹם:

Chapter 7

Exercise 1

1. young man
2. the word
3. the house
4. city
5. the cities
6. man
7. David
8. the king
9. the son
10. fathers
11. brothers
12. the mountains
13. the kings
14. peoples
15. lands
16. families
17. the animals
18. people
19. the head
20. the wine
21. the dust
22. the mountain
23. the light
24. the darkness
25. the foot

Exercise 2

1. The Lord is one.
2. And the King, Solomon, will be blessed.
3. By me kings reign.
4. A wealthy woman was there.

Chapter 8

Exercise 1

1. a wise father
2. a good king
3. a big people
4. a good son
5. good sons
6. good daughters
7. good words
8. good families
9. big cities
10. good fathers
11. a good father
12. the big house
13. the good family
14. the wise father
15. the big houses
16. the good families
17. the wise fathers

Exercise 2

1. The city is great.
2. The mother is good.
3. The man is old.
4. The house is big.
5. The woman is old.
6. The earth is good.
7. The people is big.
8. The father is good.
9. The horse is big.
10. The sons are good.

Chapter 9

Exercise 1

1. I am the man.
2. You are the daughter.
3. He is a good man.
4. It is the place.
5. You are the man.
6. We are the sons.
7. They are brothers.
8. They are the daughters.
9. I am the priest.
10. You are the queen.

Exercise 2

1. to me
2. to you (mpl)
3. to them (f)
4. to us (m or f)
5. to her
6. he kept them (f)
7. he kept you (ms)
8. he kept you (fs)

Exercise 3

1. I am the Lord.
2. It is the great city.

Chapter 10

Exercise

1. my (m and f) horse
2. their (m) horse
3. their (f) horse
4. your (fs) law
5. their (f) law
6. our (m and f) law
7. his law
8. your (mpl) law
9. her law
10. my (m and f) horses
11. your (fs) horses
12. his horses
13. your (mpl) horses
14. their (f) horses
15. my (m and f) laws
16. his laws
17. our (m and f) laws
18. your (fpl) laws
19. their (f) laws
20. their (m) laws

Chapter 11

Exercise 1

1. This is the day.
2. This is the law.
3. Holy is this place.
4. Good are these words.
5. This is the people.
6. This is the good city.
7. That is the good Covenant.
8. This is the blessing.
9. This is our horse.

Exercise 2

1. and a horse
2. and the money
3. and words
4. and the man
5. and the horses
6. and the light
7. and a king
8. and also

Exercise 3

1. These are the things which you shall do on that day.

Chapter 12

Exercise 1

1. in a family
2. like a king
3. to Moab
4. to a brother
5. like kings
6. to Jerusalem
7. in the house
8. to the city
9. in a house
10. like the king
11. in the way
12. in the mountain
13. in the land
14. to the king
15. to the man
16. in a month
17. to Samuel
18. to Edom

Exercise 2

1. from a house
2. from a man
3. from the king
4. from a man
5. from Samuel

Chapter 13

Exercise 1

1. a word of a king
2. a wife of a king
3. a king of peace
4. a man of war
5. a wife of a man
6. the man of the mountain
7. a day of peace
8. the voice of the son
9. the son of the king
10. a word of peace
11. the master of everything
12. the wife of Abraham
13. the king of Egypt
14. the daughter of David
15. the way of the king
16. a city of peace
17. the head of the youth
18. the heart of the man
19. the hand of Moses
20. all of the day

Exercise 2

1. a word of a wife of a king
2. the head of the city of Moses
3. the name of the son of Moses
4. the heart of the wife of David
5. to the mountain of the desert
6. from the hand of Moses
7. the men of the place
8. eyes of a man
9. the eyes of the king
10. the sons of the city

Exercise 3

1. You have built the house of the Lord, and the house of the King.
2. The word of the Lord is good.

Chapter 14

Exercise 1

1. 11
2. 31
3. 101
4. 122
5. 223
6. 1000
7. 214
8. 500
9. 17
10. 28

Exercise 2

1. a first woman
2. the first man
3. three sons
4. eight daughters
5. Samuel is greater than David.

Chapter 15

Exercise 1

1. he is keeping
2. they (m) are keeping
3. they (f) are keeping
4. you (fs) are keeping
5. you (ms) are keeping
6. you (mpl) are keeping
7. I (f) am keeping
8. you (fpl) are keeping

Exercise 2

1. he is keeping
2. the one who is keeping
3. the keeping man
4. it is written
5. the written one
6. the written word

Chapter 16

Exercise 1

1. he kept
2. you (fs) kept
3. the kings kept
4. we (m and f) stood
5. queens sat
6. you (f) went
7. the king went
8. the queen kept
9. you (mpl) sat

Exercise 2

1. I will keep
2. you (fs) will keep
3. the king will keep
4. the queen will keep
5. the daughters will keep
6. the kings will keep
7. and he kept
8. and he will keep

Chapter 17

Exercise

1. to keep
2. he kept
3. I (m and f) will keep
4. they (m) kept
5. you (mpl) will keep
6. you (fpl) will keep
7. Keep! (ms)
8. you (fs) kept
9. she kept
10. Keep! (fpl)
11. Keep! (fs)
12. we (m and f) will keep
13. you (fs) will keep
14. he will keep
15. you (mpl) kept
16. he is keeping
17. they (m) are keeping
18. Keep! (mpl)
19. they (f) are keeping
20. we (m and f) kept

Chapter 18

Exercise

1. I am being kept
2. he is being kept
3. you (mpl) are being kept
4. they (f) are being kept
5. I was kept
6. she was kept
7. you (fpl) were kept
8. you (ms) were kept
9. I (m or f) will be kept
10. he will be kept
11. you will be kept
    she will be kept
12. they (m) will be kept
13. Be kept! (fpl)
14. Be kept! (ms)
15. to be kept
16. you (mpl) shall be kept
17. Be kept! (fs)
18. we (f) are being kept
19. you (mpl) were kept
20. she is being kept

Chapter 19

Exercise

1. I (m) am shattering
2. we (m and f) are shattering
3. she is shattering
4. they (m) are shattering
5. you (ms) shattered
6. we (m and f) shattered
7. you (mpl) shattered
8. you (fs) shattered
9. I (m and f) will shatter
10. you will shatter
    she will shatter
11. we (m and f) will shatter
12. they (m) will shatter
13. he will shatter
14. Shatter! (ms)
    indeed shatter
15. Shatter! (fpl)
16. to shatter
17. Shatter! (mpl)
18. you (ms) are shattering
19. they (m and f) shattered

Chapter 20

Exercise

1. You (ms) are being shattered.
2. We (m) are being shattered.
3. They (f) are being shattered.
4. He is being shattered.
5. He was shattered.
6. You (mpl) were shattered.
7. You (fpl) were shattered.
8. They (m and f) were shattered.
9. We (m and f) were shattered.
10. I (m and f) was shattered.
11. You (ms) will be shattered.
    She will be shattered.
12. He will be shattered.
13. We will be shattered.
14. You (fpl) will be shattered.
    They (f) will be shattered.
15. They (m) will be shattered.
16. Indeed be shattered.
17. She is being shattered.
18. We (f) are being shattered.
19. I am being shattered.
20. She was shattered.

Chapter 21

Exercise

1. I am causing to rule
2. he is causing to rule
3. we (m) are causing to rule
4. they (f) are causing to rule
5. you (fs) caused to rule
6. she caused to rule
7. you (mpl) caused to rule
8. they (m and f) caused to rule
9. I will cause to rule
10. you (fs) will cause to rule
11. you (ms) will cause to rule
    she will cause to rule
12. we will cause to rule
13. you (fpl) will cause to rule
    they (f) will cause to rule
14. you (mpl) will cause to rule

15. Cause to rule! (fs)
16. Cause to rule! (mpl)
17. Cause to rule! (fpl)

18. to cause to rule
19. he caused to rule
20. we caused to rule

Chapter 22

Exercise

1. I (m) am being made great.
2. You (fs) are being made great.
3. We (m) are being made great.

4. You (mpl) are being made great.
5. You (ms) were made great.
6. He was made great.
7. We (m and f) were made great.
8. You (mpl) were made great.
9. They (m and f) were made great.
10. I (m and f) will be made great.

11. You (ms) will be made great. She will be made great.
12. We (m and f) will be made great.
13. You (fpl) will be made great. They (f) will be made great.
14. They (mpl) will be made great.
15. indeed be made great
16. He is being made great.
17. She is being made great.
18. You (fs) were made great.
19. They (m and f) were made great.

Chapter 23

Exercise

1. I (m) am sanctifying myself.
2. You (ms) are sanctifying yourself.
3. She is sanctifying herself.
4. We (f) are sanctifying ourselves.
5. They (f) are sanctifying themselves.
6. You (ms) sanctified yourself.
7. He sanctified himself.
8. You (mpl) sanctified yourselves.

9. Sanctify yourselves! (mpl)
10. Sanctify yourself! (ms)
11. You (fs) will sanctify yourself.
12. He will sanctify himself.
13. We (m and f) will sanctify ourselves.
14. You (fpl) will sanctify yourselves. They (f) will sanctify themselves.
15. They (m) will sanctify themselves.